A real-world independent project

By Melanie L. Bondy

Edited by Shanda Blue Easterday MFA, PhD

Printed by Data Reproductions Corporation
Auburn Hills, Michigan, U.S.A.

DEDICATION

To my Aunt Mim, a true blessing to everyone she touched. She will forever be missed.

ACKNOWLEDGMENTS

For their support and encouragement: Scott and Brendan Bondy, Richard and Marilyn Bondy and Alvina Betka.

To the principals who believed in me: Sara O'Hara, Laura Holbert and Kurt Swearingen.

To the L'Anse Creuse Public Schools superintendent, Dr. DiAnne Pellerin, who recognized the benefits of this program and encouraged me to present it outside of my school and district.

To the students who gave me the honor of being able to share their projects with others: Elizabeth Boschma, Kristen Boschma, Adrianna Katsimpalis, Ariel Katsimpalis, Marissa Krause, Lauren Marino, Kelsey Nucci, Nicole Paul, Sarah Trerice, Brooke Will and Shuda Jarobe.

To my graphic artist, Michael Bartello, for his exceptional talent, ideas, friendship and eagerness to help.

To my editor, Shanda Blue Easterday, for her hard work, dedication and belief in the Envision program.

To my additional graphic artist, Eric Howes, for his excellent work ethic, ideas and flexibility.

To my dear friends, Maggie Elms and Gretchen DeVisser, for their continued help and constant support.

Copyright © 2012 Melanie L. Bondy

All rights reserved. Unless otherwise noted, no part of this book or program components may be reproduced, stored in a retrieval system or transmitted in any form or by any means, electronic, mechanical, photocopied, recorded or otherwise without express written permission of the publisher, except for brief quotations in a review.

Reproduction of any part of this program for more than one teacher is strictly forbidden.

Permission is given to individual teachers to print and photocopy forms included in the appendices of this book for individual classroom work only, provided that the permissions line on each form remains. Customizing, printing, photocopying or other reproduction of these materials for other teachers, an entire school, school system, web site or schooling network is strictly forbidden.

Bondy, Melanie L.

Envision, Party Plan: Melanie L. Bondy: edited by Shanda Blue Easterday MFA, PhD.

Cover and book design by Michael Bartello, seesponge.com.

Spanish translation and editing by Bella Lile and Laura McCarthy.

Printed in the United States of America, Data Reproductions Corporation.

Referenced with permission: *Taxonomy of Educational Objectives: Book 1: Cognitive Domain*, Benjamin S. Bloom, Ed. Copyright © 1956, 1984. Pearson Allyn and Bacon, Boston, MA.

Mind Vine Press, LLC
6818 Calm Meadow Drive, Frisco, TX 75035
www.mindvinepress.com
ISBN: 978-0-9835533-0-4

TABLE OF CONTENTS

Author Letter: A Solution to Providing Real-World Challenge 1

Program Introduction: The Envision Experience 3
• What is Envision? • What type of class can use Envision? • Which students can participate in Envision? • Are there recommended sequences and grade levels for the various Envision projects? • How are the student materials organized? • How are the teacher materials organized? • What additional materials does the program include? • What is Bloom's Taxonomy of Educational Objectives? • What distinguishes each of Bloom's levels? • What is Envision's connection to Bloom's Taxonomy? • What are the other available Envision programs and projects?

Teacher Instruction Guide for Project Implementation

Step 1: Plan and Prepare for the Project 9
Step 2: Student Introduction 12
Step 3: Project Implementation 17
Step 4: Checkpoint Meetings 22
Step 5: Prepare for the Project Expo and the Classroom Presentations 25
Step 6: Conduct the Classroom Presentations 32
Step 7: Classroom Expo and Student Self-Assessment 35
Step 8: Final Preparation for the Project Expo 37
Step 9: The Project Expo 38
Step 10: Conclusion, Teacher Assessment and Student Review. 38

Appendices

Appendix 1: Party Plan Forms 40
Appendix 2: Party Plan Resource Cards for Students 94
Appendix 3: Spanish Translations of Parent Forms 101
Appendix 4: Additional Information 106
Appendix 5: Party Plan Resource Cards for the Classroom 108

AUTHOR LETTER: A SOLUTION TO PROVIDING REAL-WORLD CHALLENGE

A SOLUTION TO PROVIDING REAL-WORLD CHALLENGE

Teaching has always meant more than presenting lessons, assigning homework and grading papers. Today, educators are asked to micromanage a host of objectives and topics that stretch far beyond the standard core curriculum. While tackling these new responsibilities, teachers must still contend with the task of educating an often under-served population of students whose needs are substantially different from those of most of their classmates: the gifted, or any students needing extra challenge.

As a teacher, I struggled to provide the best education I could for all my students. In my first class of thirty-five students I had five students who were in a cluster group for the gifted. I also had several other students who were not formally labeled as gifted, but often needed extra challenge. These students often tested out of lessons or accelerated through lessons much quicker than the remainder of the class. I worked long hours to find and create innovative lessons, and then endeavored to adapt each lesson to accommodate any students who needed the extra challenge.

I was fortunate, in that first year of teaching, to take part in a one-year training program for teaching the gifted, and I learned of the available strategies for teaching gifted students. I looked forward to these strategies helping my students excel in school, and I became motivated and energized to utilize them right away.

As I began implementing the techniques I had learned, which included supplying research projects, explorations, logic exercises and high-level thinking games, I believed these new exercises were sufficiently challenging my students. After only about a week with each new activity, however, I noticed that the activities were becoming repetitive and mundane. The logic problems offered different scenarios, but all employed the same type of thinking. Once the students understood the first few logic problems, solving the rest became mechanical. In addition, the problems had little or no relationship to the students' personal lives.

The research projects and explorations I had so hopefully adopted proved, in a classroom setting, to be haphazardly grouped, difficult to manage, extremely broad and unclear in their requirements and too subject-specific to allow for much curriculum flexibility. They were also not deep enough to engage the students for more than a few weeks.

Of additional significance, I found that I had no valuable way of assessing—and therefore promoting—student advancement. The logic exercises, for example, included answer keys, but the keys offered no means to evaluate the levels of thinking associated with solving the problems. Answers were simply right or wrong. Similarly, the thinking games, explorations and research projects all defied useful assessment, leaving me to guess at where my students were and where they were poised to go. A colorful portfolio showcasing the end products of various broad activities and repetitive projects is a poor substitute for a thorough, convincing record of demonstrable advancement in high-level thinking.

Although my students were enjoying their new extra activities, they were, in fact, being little more than entertained. At this point, though frustrated from researching and prepping materials that had proved to be of such limited value, I was unwilling to accept that "the best available" was the best I could offer my students. I grew more determined than ever to find a solution to this nagging problem.

To solve the problem, I developed Envision, a series of objective-based independent projects that is exciting and challenging, that leads students through the highest levels of thinking and that appeals to diverse interests by having deep roots in reality. Because Envision projects draw on all subject areas, students can work on their projects at any time of the day, during any class period, and still be connected to the general work of the class.

Of special importance to me is that each student's progress is subject to clear, consistent, unambiguous assessment at predetermined stages from start to finish. Envision is ambitious enough in its depth and scope to engage, challenge and reward students all year long. Finally, Envision is a program that students work on with minimal oversight, which encourages independent learning and, as a practical concern, allows more time for the teacher to address other classroom needs.

PROGRAM INTRODUCTION:
THE ENVISION EXPERIENCE

THE ENVISION EXPERIENCE

What is Envision?

Envision is a real-world independent study program for students who are not sufficiently challenged by the standard curriculum. Each multidisciplinary project is designed to last about one quarter of the school year with students working an average of thirty minutes per day.

What type of class can use Envision?

Intended to complement or replace the standard curriculum for any students needing extra challenge, the projects integrate advanced academic study with real-world topics and problem solving. Since the projects are not subject-specific, drawing as they do from all disciplines, they can be integrated easily into any type of classroom setting. The Envision program is flexible enough to be used in a regular education classroom that has gifted and talented students or does not identify gifted students, in a classroom of only gifted students or in a classroom where gifted students are pulled out for periods of time to be served.

Which students can participate in Envision?

Students who participate in the program are those who are gifted, talented or simply need extra challenge.

> **IMPORTANT!**
>
> Almost positively, especially after seeing the first projects completed, your non-Envision students will want to participate in the Envision projects. Allowing all students to participate in Envision will not only excite and motivate everyone about school, but will also make you feel good knowing that you are providing the best opportunities for all of your students. Any students can take on the Envision challenges and will probably surprise you with their level of enthusiasm and learning.
>
> Allowing all students to participate in the projects may require some extra work on your part. You may choose, for instance, to modify the Student Instruction Guides, you will have extra photocopying to do and you will need to hold a larger Project Expo. Expanding participation to all students, however, will greatly reward both you and them.

Are there recommended sequences and grade levels for the various projects?

While any one Envision project can be taught independently from the others, the program is most effective when multiple projects are accomplished over the course of a school year. The projects are designed in a way that teachers can implement a new one each quarter of the school year, or approximately every ten to eleven weeks. Of course, depending on scheduling, some teachers may be able to accomplish more, some less. On average, to see optimal results, students spend about thirty minutes per day for approximately nine weeks (the tenth being the presentations and expo week) on each project.

The projects were originally developed as grade-level sets, with each set containing a series of four projects. The first project in each grade-level set is designed to familiarize students with a new style of learning, and, for that reason, is slightly less demanding than the other three. The second project in each series is more challenging in that it involves students in numerous tasks associated with cognitive skills higher up on the scale included in Benjamin S. Bloom's Taxonomy of Educational Objectives (Bloom, 1956, 1984). The third is typically the most academically rigorous of all, requiring more intellectual work at the highest levels of thinking than any of the other projects. The fourth and final project of each, though not as critically demanding as the second and third, allows students a great deal of intellectual and creative freedom, thereby challenging them in ways the other three projects do not.

The available grade-level sets and project descriptions are at the end of this introductory section. Most Envision projects can easily be taken up or down a grade level without making changes. Some can be taken up or down more than one grade level. Consider the first and last projects in each set the easiest to take down a grade level, and the middle two projects in each set the easiest to take up a grade level.

THE ENVISION EXPERIENCE

How are the student materials organized?

Throughout the Envision project, students will receive sections of a Student Instruction Guide containing the objectives for the project. The instruction guide allows students to work on their projects independently, guiding them step-by-step through the objectives. Students also receive Project Organizers that correspond to certain objectives in their student guide. Each organizer provides a framework for its corresponding objective. For every Envision project, students are guided to create a comprehensive portfolio, a formal classroom presentation and an exhibit presented at an Envision project expo.

If students need additional guidance along the way, a set of important Student Resource Cards is included and offers a wide range of supplemental instruction. The resource cards offer definitions, helpful tips and visual examples for certain tasks listed on the Student Instruction Guide.

Though the teacher introduces the program and is available for periodic guidance, encouragement and assessment, the Student Instruction Guide, organizers and resource cards enable students to work largely on their own and at their own pace. This structure encourages independent learning for students, while allowing the teacher ample time to attend to his or her regular responsibilities.

At the completion of each project, students receive a Student Self-Assessment that gives them the opportunity to reflect on and assess their work.

How are the teacher materials organized?

Following this introduction, there is a Teacher Instruction Guide. The Teacher Instruction Guide is also presented in a step-by-step format and explains project implementation from start to finish. It includes detailed instructions, examples and references to all the forms and materials teachers will use along the way.

In addition to the Teacher Instruction Guide is the project forms appendix. The appendix contains all the letters, charts, invitations, signs, certificates and assessments needed to complete the Envision program. These reproducible forms are provided in order of use.

What additional materials does the program include?

In addition to this manual, the package contains the Student Resource Cards previously discussed, Spanish translations of parent materials and a specially designed CD. The CD contains all the PDF files of forms, in color and with typeable fields. There is also useful information for both teachers and students at mindvinepress.com.

What is Bloom's Taxonomy of Educational Objectives?

Benjamin S. Bloom's Taxonomy of Educational Objectives is a model that presents thinking as occurring at six levels, and ranks those levels from the least complex, or the lowest level, to the most abstract, or the highest level. The type of cognition that occurs at any given level distinguishes that level from the others. At the lower end, in Bloom's original 1956 Taxonomy, are Knowledge, Comprehension and Application, in rising order. At the higher end are Analysis, Synthesis and, ultimately, Evaluation.

Over the decades, however, educators who have worked with Bloom's Taxonomy have made a significant change to the hierarchy of cognitive activities. In most educational circles, Synthesis now ranks above Evaluation as the highest level, making Evaluation the second highest.

THE ENVISION EXPERIENCE

What distinguishes each of the Bloom's levels?

A practical way to understand these six levels of thinking and how they relate to one another is to know the cognitive activity that occurs at each level, and the skills associated with each cognitive activity.

Knowledge, at the lowest cognitive level, involves recalling something previously encountered, but does not involve understanding or applying that knowledge. Related skills include memorizing, listing, defining, quoting, naming, simple labeling, locating and knowing who, when, where, what and how many.

Comprehension requires that a student understand knowledge, such as the nature of an important event, for example, rather than merely when and where the event occurred. Comprehension does not, however, require the student to apply that knowledge to other knowledge, such as a similar event. Related skills include summarizing, describing, estimating, interpreting, outlining, collecting, demonstrating and understanding how as opposed to simply how many.

Application occurs when a student uses learned knowledge to solve new problems in new situations. Related skills include calculating, solving, experimenting, resolving and answering.

Analysis, the first of the three highest-level activities, occurs when a student dissects a concept or object into its component parts and examines those parts separately and in relation to one another or to the whole. Related skills include separating, ordering, diagramming, classifying, dividing, comparing, contrasting and finding patterns.

Evaluation means offering an opinion on the value of information, events or concepts based on specific criteria. Related skills include assessing, ranking, persuading, judging, supporting and refuting.

Synthesis, widely considered the most abstract kind of thinking, occurs when a student can restructure the parts of a whole into something new. The ability to create something new from what has been learned requires a thorough understanding of the subject matter, an understanding of its applications and its parts and an evaluative opinion regarding each part's importance and relevance to the whole. Related skills include integrating, revising, rearranging, substituting, designing, composing, building, organizing, interviewing, hypothesizing and inventing.

> **IMPORTANT!**
> The levels described above are cumulative; for example, the highest level of thinking, Synthesis, incorporates all other levels of thinking: Knowledge, Comprehension, Application, Analysis and Evaluation. Please keep this in mind when reviewing the Envision project's connection to Bloom's Taxonomy discussed below.

What is Envision's connection to Bloom's Taxonomy?

As mentioned above, each Envision project includes a specific, varied set of advanced objectives that have been carefully selected and organized according to Benjamin S. Bloom's widely accepted and updated Taxonomy of Educational Objectives. Although the projects incorporate all levels of thinking, the bulk of the objectives for each project focuses on exercising the three highest levels.

If you would like to see this project's connection to the Bloom's Taxonomy levels, go to the beginning of the project appendix.

THE ENVISION EXPERIENCE

What are the other available Envision programs and projects?

In addition to Envision Singles, Mind Vine Press offers grade-level sets of Envision programs. Each Envision Complete Grade Level Program comes with the Envision teacher guide and four complete projects that include pre-cut Student Resource Cards, teacher forms and customizable CD. The Complete Grade Level Programs also come with five color posters and a bulletin board banner.

Complete Envision Programs Available

Envision: Grade 3 Complete Program

 Pet Parade: Choose and research a pet to adopt or purchase in the future.

 Giving Journey: Choose a gift for someone and create a plan to work for it.

 Discovery Science: Design and conduct a scientific experiment.

 Curiosity Expedition: Research an exciting topic of your choice.

Envision: Grade 4 Complete Program

 Design a complete, personalized dream backyard using one acre of land.

 Acquire an awareness of an environmental issue and have a voice in the matter.

 Interact and learn within the community while planning and performing a service.

 Develop a detailed plan of healthy habits by which to live.

THE ENVISION EXPERIENCE

Envision: Grade 5 Complete Program

 Plan every aspect of a trip from start to finish within a specified budget.

 Research a career and all of the education required to accomplish this major life goal.

 Plan personal finances and purchases based on the starting salary of a chosen career.

 Thoroughly investigate and report on a meaningful and relevant topic of choice.

Envision Singles Available

Envision Single: Career Aspiration, Appropriate for Grades 5-8

 Research a career and all of the education required to accomplish this major life goal.

Envision Single: Backyard Getaway, Appropriate for Grades 4-7

 Design a complete, personalized dream backyard using one acre of land.

Envision Single: Pet Parade, Appropriate for Grades 3-6

 Choose and research a pet to adopt or purchase in the future.

Envision Single: Party Plan, Appropriate for Grades 2-3

 Plan a themed party to celebrate a special event.

For detailed descriptions and ordering information, please visit mindvinepress.com.

TEACHER INSTRUCTION GUIDE FOR PROJECT IMPLEMENTATION

TEACHER INSTRUCTION GUIDE

You are now ready to begin implementing the Envision program in your classroom. This Teacher Instruction Guide serves as a comprehensive checklist for every step necessary to achieve success. The instruction guide is based on a school year comprised of four ten-week quarters. Please note that the ten-week schedule is flexible.

IMPORTANT!
Since the format for each Envision project is the same, you may use this instruction guide for any Envision project, should you decide to implement more than one project per school year. Note that upper grade-level projects allow teachers to provide the entire Student Instruction Guide at the beginning of the project. There are no student organizers included or needed with upper grade-level programs.

 Every step in the Teacher Instruction Guide includes detailed instructions and visual examples.

STEP 1
Plan and Prepare for the Project

The first form, the Teacher Planning Guide, allows you to plan every stage of each project from start to finish. Setting dates and times for project events well in advance will guarantee the best possible outcome.

Students should be given an entire quarter, or about ten weeks, to work on and complete one project. This ten-week period can be slightly flexible, give or take a week, as needed.

Note: The Teacher Instruction Guide walks you through the entire project implementation process. Forms you will use are included with each step in the order they are needed. It is best to do the photocopying as you proceed with each step, rather than copying everything up front, since many forms will need to be filled in prior to photocopying. Located in Appendix 1 is a Teacher Copy Chart that lists each form you will need, when you will need it and how many copies you will need.

TEACHER INSTRUCTION GUIDE

1.1 Copy one Teacher Planning Guide.

1.2 Use the guidelines below, along with the chart that follows, to direct you in filling out your personal Teacher Planning Guide. It may be helpful to start with Week 10 and work in reverse.

Week 1 Preparation, Introduction, Implementation:
- 30 minutes outside of class for initial planning and preparing (Steps 1.1-1.2).
- 15 minutes outside of class to prepare for Project Introduction (2.1-2.3).
- 20 minutes of class time for Project Introduction (2.4-2.7). The Project Introduction should be presented at least one day prior to Project Implementation (below).
- 20 minutes outside of class to prepare for Project Implementation (3.1-3.6).
- 30 minutes of class time for Project Implementation (3.7-3.16).

Weeks 2, 4 and 6 Additional Student Materials:
- 10 minutes of class time to distribute the week's section of the Student Instruction Guide and its corresponding organizers.

Weeks 3, 5 and 7 Checkpoint Meetings:
- 10 minutes outside of class to prepare for the Checkpoint Meetings (4.1-4.2).
- 10 minutes of class time to distribute Checkpoint Organizers (4.3-4.6). Distribute the Checkpoint Organizers two to three days prior to the Checkpoint Meetings (below).
- 10 minutes of class time, per every five to six Envision students, to conduct Checkpoint Meetings (4.7-4.12).
- 10 minutes of class time to distribute the week's section of the Student Instruction Guide and its corresponding organizers.

Week 8 Preparation, Invitations:
- 10 minutes outside of class to prepare for the Project Expo (5.1-5.2).
- 10 minutes of class time to Invite Families to the Project Expo (5.3-5.4).
- 60 minutes outside of class to continue preparation for the Project Expo (5.5-5.11).
- 10 minutes of class time to distribute the final section of the Student Instruction Guide and its corresponding organizers.

Week 9 Preparation, Classroom Presentations, Classroom Expo, Student Self-Assessment:
- 30 minutes outside of class, plus an optional store trip, to prepare for the Classroom Presentations and Project Expo (5.12-5.15). Prepare two to three days prior to Classroom Presentations (below).
- 5 minutes of class time, per Envision student, to conduct the Classroom Presentations (6A.1-6A.13 or 6B.1-6B.12). The Classroom Presentations should be on the same day and during the same time block as the Classroom Expo and Student Self-Assessment (below).
- 5 minutes of class time, per each Envision student, plus an additional 10 minutes for the Classroom Expo and Student Self-Assessment (7A.1-7A.9 or 7B.1-7B.10).

Week 10 Final Preparation, Project Expo, Teacher Assessment:
- 45 minutes outside of class to complete Final Preparation for the Project Expo (8.1-8.8). This preparation must be done on the day of the Project Expo.
- 60 minutes of class time to conduct the Project Expo (9.1-9.4). Scheduling the expo in the evening ensures better attendance by parents.
- Photo printing time and 10 minutes outside of class per each Envision student, for the Conclusion and Teacher Assessment (10.1-10.7).
- 15 minutes of class time for Student Review (10.8-10.9).

TEACHER PLANNING GUIDE

Events scheduled with the class are in black.

Week	Event (Step Numbers)	Time Required
1	Plan and Prepare for the Project (1.1-1.2)	30 min.
	Prepare for Project Introduction (2.1-2.3)	15 min.
	Project Introduction (2.4-2.7) (day prior to Project Implementation)	20 min.
	Prepare for Project Implementation (3.1-3.6)	20 min.
	Project Implementation (3.7-3.16)	30 min.
2	Distribute this week's section of the Student Instruction Guide (SIG) and its corresponding Organizers.	10 min.
3	Prepare for the Checkpoint Meetings (4.1-4.2)	10 min.
	Distribute SIG/Organizers, then Checkpoint Organizers (4.3-4.6) 2-3 days prior to Meetings	10 min.
	Checkpoint Meetings (4.7-4.12) (For every 5-6 Envision students)	10 min.
4	Distribute this week's section of the Student Instruction Guide and its corresponding Organizers.	10 min.
5	Prepare for the Checkpoint Meetings (4.1-4.2)	10 min.
	Distribute SIG/Organizers, then Checkpoint Organizers (4.3-4.6) 2-3 days prior to Meetings	10 min.
	Checkpoint Meetings (4.7-4.12) (For every 5-6 Envision students)	10 min.
6	Distribute this week's section of the Student Instruction Guide and its corresponding organizers.	10 min.
7	Prepare for the Checkpoint Meetings (4.1-4.2)	10 min.
	Distribute SIG/Organizers, then Checkpoint Organizers (4.3-4.6) 2-3 days prior to Meetings	10 min.
	Checkpoint Meetings (4.7-4.12) (For every 5-6 Envision students)	10 min.
8	Prepare for the Project Expo (5.1-5.2)	10 min.
	Distribute SIG/Organizers, and Invite Families to the Project Expo (5.3-5.4)	10 min.
	Prepare for the Project Expo Cont. (5.5-5.11)	60 min.
9	Prepare for Classroom Presentations and the Project Expo (5.12-5.15) 2-3 days prior to Presentations	30 min. (+ store: optional)
	Classroom Presentations (6A.1-6A.13 or 6B.1-6B.12) Same time-block as Classroom Expo and Student Self-Assessment	5 min. per Envision student
	Classroom Expo and Student Self-Assessment (7A.1-7A.9 or 7B.1-7B.10)	5 min. per Envision student + 10 min.
10	Final Preparation for the Project Expo (8.1-8.8) the day of the Expo	45 min.
	Project Expo (9.1-9.4) Preferably in evening to ensure parent availability	60 min.
	Conclusion and Teacher Assessment (10.1-10.7)	Photo printing + 10 min./student
	Student Review (10.8-10.9)	15 min.

TEACHER INSTRUCTION GUIDE

STEP 2
Student Introduction

> **IMPORTANT!**
> If you would like to see this project's specific connections to the Bloom's Taxonomy levels, please see the beginning of Appendix 1.

Prepare for Project Introduction:

2.1 Make one copy of the Parent Envision Introduction Letter, one of the Parent Project Introduction Letter, one of the Student Project Introduction Letter and one of the Student Instruction Guide.

2.2 Using the information from your Teacher Planning Guide, complete the Parent Envision Introduction Letter, Parent Project Introduction Letter and Student Project Introduction Letter.

> **IMPORTANT!**
> When completing the information on the forms, remember that there are two options:
> 1. You may choose to photocopy the form from the appendix and fill in the blanks by hand.
> OR
> 2. You may use the CD to type in the blanks, then print the form in color or black and white.

2.3 Copy a completed Parent Envision Introduction Letter, and a Parent Project Introduction Letter for each student. Do not make multiple copies of the Student Introduction Letter or Student Instruction Guide at this time. You will need only one of each of these right now.

Project Introduction:

2.4 Bring your students together and, referring to the Parent Envision Introduction Letter, give them an overview of the Envision Program.

2.5 Read aloud the Student Introduction Letter to give students an overview of the project. Refer to the Student Instruction Guide to highlight some of the project tasks.

2.6 To each student, hand one Parent Envision Introduction Letter to take home. Explain that the bottom portion of it contains an Envision Permission Form that the parent should sign, detach and return to you as soon as possible.

2.7 To each student, also hand one Parent Project Introduction Letter to take home.

 introduction letter

EXAMPLE

Dear Parent(s),

I am happy to inform you that your child has been invited to participate in an advanced academic program called Envision. I am sending you this letter to explain the program and ask for your permission to include your child in this special opportunity.

Envision is an exciting program designed for students who are not sufficiently challenged by the standard grade-level curriculum. The focus of the program is on developing high-level critical thinking and creativity. It guides students through real-world-based projects that encourage them to envision how they might achieve their personal goals in the future.

Your child is being invited to participate in the Party Plan project, which allows students to plan a themed party to celebrate a special event.

Students will work on Envision during class time, free time and at home.

To give permission for your child to participate in Envision, simply sign the Envision Permission Form at the bottom of this letter, detach it and return the form to me. If you want your child to participate in Envision, please read the attached Parent Party Plan Introduction Letter. The letter introduces you to the project, informs you of important dates and requests permission for your child's continued participation.

Envision promises to be a wonderful learning opportunity for your child. I look forward to hearing from you. Please feel free to contact me if you have any questions.

Sincerely,
Mrs. Bondy
269-978-7227 · bondyme@school.org

---

envision permission form

Please fill out this section, detach and return as soon as possible.   Date: *September 6, 2XXX*

❏ I have read the Parent Envision Introduction Letter and give my child permission to participate in the Envision program.

❏ I have read the Parent Envision Introduction Letter and do not give my child permission to participate in the Envision program.

Child's Name: *Alyssa Good*   Parent's Signature: *Joanne Good*

parent party plan introduction letter

Dear Parent(s),

Welcome to Party Plan, a project from the Envision program that will challenge and inspire your child. Party Plan will immediately engage your child as its challenge is to plan a themed party to celebrate a special event.

For this project, your child will choose an event to celebrate and a theme to incorporate into his or her party. Next, your child will create a party banner and read books related to the party theme. Your child will also create a party game, craft, invitation, map, food and drink budget poster, serving area illustration and much more. Most of these materials will be collected in a portfolio. Next, your child will design and create an exhibit that captures and conveys the highlights of his or her Party Plan project. Last, your child will present his or her project to the class.

A weekly Student Instruction Guide will be provided to guide your child, step by step, through this process. The Instruction Guide is a comprehensive list of project requirements and is designed to engage higher-level thinking. Along with this guide, your child will receive project organizers that correspond with certain objective requirements. The guide also references helpful resource cards that provide additional explanations, ideas, tips and directions. There will be a set of these cards to which your child may refer in our classroom.

Party Plan is designed to be worked on independently during class time, free time and at home. By scheduling several Checkpoint Meeting dates throughout the project, I will be able to monitor each student's progress. On these dates, I will meet with each student to discuss accomplishments and plan goals for the next checkpoint. I will also address any difficulties students might be having.

Party Plan will conclude with a celebratory Project Expo. The expo will be your child's opportunity to share his or her finished project with family, friends and other guests. Closer to the Project Expo date, you will receive a detailed invitation.

Dates to Remember:

Checkpoint 1: September 18, 2XXX

Checkpoint 2: October 2, 2XXX

Checkpoint 3: October 16, 2XXX

Classroom Presentation: November 1, 2XXX

Party Plan Expo: November 7, 2XXX 6:30 - 7:30 pm

Sincerely,
Mrs. Bondy
269-978-7227 · bondyme@school.org

student party plan introduction letter

Dear Student,

Welcome to Party Plan! This project will guide you to plan a party that celebrates an event of your choice.

Party Plan begins with choosing an event and a party theme. You will also create a party banner, party game, craft, invitation, map, poster and much more.

You will store your Party Plan materials in a portfolio as you complete them. You will also build a display and share your project in class. At the end of the project, there will be a Project Expo. This is an event that will celebrate your hard work with family and friends.

You will work on Party Plan at school, during your free time and at home. Mostly, you will be expected to work on your own. We will have Checkpoint Meetings to discuss how your project is coming along and to provide help if needed. Between the checkpoints, you may talk about your project with other Envision students.

The attached Student Instruction Guide contains the first week's requirements for your Party Plan Project. The attached organizers will help you complete some of the requirements. There are also resource cards in our classroom that will help you complete your project successfully.

Dates to Remember:

Checkpoint 1: _September 18, 2XXX_

Checkpoint 2: _October 2, 2XXX_

Checkpoint 3: _October 16, 2XXX_

Classroom Presentation: _November 1, 2XXX_

Party Plan Expo: _November 7, 2XXX 6:30 - 7:30 pm_

You are now ready to begin thinking about your Party Plan. Good luck and have fun!

Sincerely,

Mrs. Bondy
269-978-7227 · bondyme@school.org

STUDENT INSTRUCTION GUIDE

EXAMPLE

Resource cards are available when you see a Party Plan icon 🎉. Party Plan Resource cards give you helpful information and examples. Also be sure to visit www.mindvinepress.com, other trustworthy Internet sites and library materials for more help.

WEEK 1: Party Type
Total Possible Points: 9 out of 100 total possible for the project.

1. 🎉 **Party Type Balloon Brainstorm** (2 points): Think about different events in life that you might like to celebrate. Using your Balloon Brainstorm organizer (attached), write various types of parties you might like to have to celebrate these events. Record one type of party on each balloon, using at least five of the balloons. You will also use this organizer for the next step.

2. **Party Type Balloon Color Ranking** (3 points): Choose three different colors of crayons, pencils or markers. Now choose one of those colors for your best ideas, a second color for your second choice ideas and a third color for your least favorite ideas. Record them on your Balloon Brainstorm organizer. Color each balloon on your Balloon Brainstorm organizer according to your color key. Leave a small amount of white around the words in your balloons so they can be read. To help make your coloring decisions, think about why you might enjoy one party more than another. You will also use this organizer for the next step.

3. **Party Type Balloon Choice** (1 point): Read your Best Idea colored balloons and from those, choose the party idea that you think would be the most exciting to plan. On your Balloon Brainstorm organizer, outline your party choice balloon with a new color that makes it stand out. This will be the party you plan for this project. Include your finished Balloon Brainstorm organizer as the first page in your portfolio.

4. 🎉 **Computer-Created Bullet Point Reasons** (3 points): Use the computer and title a new document, "I chose this party because..." Next, use bullet points to list at least four reasons you chose the party you did. You may also include reasons for not choosing your other party ideas. Include this as the second page in your portfolio.

TEACHER INSTRUCTION GUIDE

STEP 3
Project Implementation

Prepare for Project Implementation:

The Student Commitment Contract mentioned below ensures that students and their parents understand and are accountable for project work time and Checkpoint Meeting expectations. It creates a formal commitment to these expectations and an understanding that students could lose their Envision privileges if they do not follow them. It also reminds students and parents of important project dates.

3.1 Copy one Teacher Forms Checklist and one Student Commitment Contract.

3.2 Fill in the Envision student names on the Teacher Forms Checklist and set it aside for later use.

3.3 Using the event dates from your Teacher Planning Guide, complete the Student Commitment Contract.

3.4 Make a copy of the completed Student Commitment Contract for each Envision student.

3.5 Copy a completed Student Project Introduction Letter, the first week's section of the Student Instruction Guide and its corresponding organizer for each of your Envision students. Staple the Student Project Introduction Letter, the guide and the organizer together as a packet, placing the introduction letter on top.

3.6 Decide on a specific location to keep the Project Resource Cards for the Classroom found in Appendix 5. These cards can be removed from this book, cut apart and stored in the classroom for student use. Securing them together with a ring is highly recommended.

> **Note:**
> You may also want to copy the pages of smaller-sized resource cards in Appendix 2 to include with the student materials each week. This is not necessary, since there is the classroom set of resource cards, but it may be helpful to students when they work on Envision outside of the classroom.

TEACHER FORMS CHECKLIST

EXAMPLE

use this checklist to record forms submitted by the students

student name	envision permission form	student commitment contract	student checkpoint organizer 1	student checkpoint organizer 2	student checkpoint organizer 3	expo invitation response number attending special equip. needed
1. Eian	✓					
2. Alysssa	✓					
3. Brian	✓					
4. Alex	✓					
5. Morgan	✓					
6. Brendan	✓					
7. Ella	✓					
8. Teagan	✓					
9. Earl	✓					
10.						
11.						
12.						
13.						
14.						
15.						
16.						
17.						
18.						
19.						
20.						
21.						
22.						
23.						
24.						
25.						

STUDENT COMMITMENT CONTRACT

expectations

project work time

I agree to:
- be responsible for following my Student Instruction Guide to do my work.
- keep track of all my project materials.
- work hard on Envision without disturbing others.
- save my unanswered questions until my teacher is free to talk.

checkpoint meetings

I will come prepared with:
- my Student Instruction Guide.
- my completed Student Checkpoint Organizer.
- all of my project materials.

important dates and times

Checkpoint 1: *September 18, 2XXX*

Checkpoint 2: *October 2, 2XXX*

Checkpoint 3: *October 16, 2XXX*

Classroom Presentation: *November 1, 2XXX*

Party Plan Expo: *November 7, 2XXX*
6:30 - 7:30 pm

signatures

I agree to:
- meet expectations on the dates listed above.
- complete each of the project requirements to the best of my ability.
- bring my project work to school each day so that I can work on it during extra time.
- take my project work from school each night so that I can work on it at home.

I understand that this Envision project is a special opportunity, and that if I do not meet the above expectations, I may be asked to return to regular classroom activities.

Student Signature: *Alyssa Good* Date: *September 6, 2XXX*

Parent Signature: *Joanne Good* Date: *September 6, 2XXX*

Please return this contract by: *September 7, 2XXX*

THEME IDEA LABELS — EXAMPLE

 COMPUTER-CREATED BULLET POINT REASONS

 PARTY TYPE BALLOON BRAINSTORM

EXAMPLES

People have parties for many reasons. Common types of parties are for holidays or celebrations such as birthday parties. Some people like to have creative types of parties such as a party to raise money for a cause or a party to celebrate an event like losing a first tooth.

Your party can be a common type of party or a creative type of party. Brainstorm party ideas that are meaningful to you and that you might have fun planning. Try to come up with many ideas so that your brain has a chance to be creative and you will have a great experience planning your party.

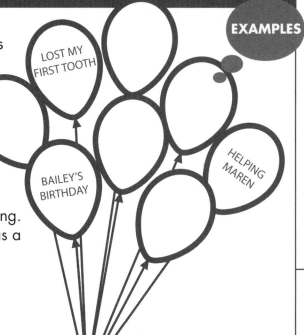

TEACHER INSTRUCTION GUIDE

Project Implementation:

3.7 Use your Teacher Forms Checklist (Step 3.1) to record each signed Envision Permission Form (distributed in Step 2.6) that is returned to you.

3.8 Distribute a Student Commitment Contract (Step 3.4) to each of your Envision students.

3.9 Review the contract with your students and answer any questions they have.

3.10 Ask each student to sign the contract, thereby agreeing to its expectations.

3.11 Direct students to take their Student Commitment Contracts home to be signed by a parent and returned to you as soon as possible.

3.12 Distribute a student packet (Step 3.5) to each of your contracted Envision students.

3.13 Read the Student Introduction Letter and review the remainder of the student packet materials together.

3.14 Share two to three resource cards with the students and explain how they correspond to particular requirements on the Student Instruction Guide. Show students where the resource cards will be kept.

IMPORTANT!
Stress to students that the Student Instruction Guide gives only the essentials for the tasks, allowing for student creativity. The resource cards, however, are available to lend additional support by supplying definitions, explanations, tips and visual examples.

3.15 Direct students to keep their materials in a safe, handy place such as a separately labeled folder or binder. Let them know that they can now work on the project at school, during extra time and at home. Tell them it is their responsibility to bring their project materials back and forth each day.

3.16 Allow students to begin using available class time to work on Envision.

Note: Record the receipt of the signed Student Commitment Contracts on the Teacher Forms Checklist as they are returned.

TEACHER INSTRUCTION GUIDE

STEP 4
Checkpoint Meetings

Although Envision is an independent study program, your interaction and guidance are crucial to each student's success. The checkpoint process assures students that they will have a scheduled time to receive your personal attention. It also allows them to share their accomplishments to date and ask any questions they may have. At each Checkpoint Meeting, you can assess progress and lend support and direction, encouraging the students to stay on track to meet upcoming deadlines. To help schedule and run your checkpoints smoothly, complete the following steps.

> **IMPORTANT!**
> You will revisit this section (Step 4) each time you plan to conduct a Checkpoint Meeting.

Prepare for Checkpoint Meetings:

4.1 Copy a Student Checkpoint Organizer for each of your Envision students.

4.2 Copy one Teacher Checkpoint Record and fill in your Envision student names.

Distribute Checkpoint Organizers:

4.3 Distribute the Student Checkpoint Organizers to your Envision students. Have each student fill in his or her name, the upcoming Checkpoint Date and party information.

4.4 Explain to the students that in a few days you will be meeting with them to discuss their projects. Explain that they will each need to complete the Student Checkpoint Organizer and bring it on that day.

4.5 Read through the organizer with them and answer any questions.

4.6 Direct the students to complete their organizer over the next few days and bring it to the Checkpoint Meeting.

Checkpoint Meetings:

4.7 While your non-Envision students are working, ask a group of five to six Envision students to meet with you for a Checkpoint Meeting. Remind them to bring their completed Student Checkpoint Organizers, Student Instruction Guides and project materials.

4.8 Using the Student Checkpoint Organizers, allow each student to respond to each question. Ask students to expand on their answers when necessary. Offer suggestions and assistance where needed.

4.9 Use your Teacher Checkpoint Record to record any notes you wish to make.

4.10 Conclude the meeting by collecting the Student Checkpoint Organizers to keep for your records.

4.11 Keep your Teacher Checkpoint Record for use at all Checkpoint Meetings and for your records.

4.12 Direct the first group of students to return to their seats and ask your next group of five to six Envision students to meet with you for a Checkpoint Meeting.

Repeat Steps 4.7 through 4.12 until all your Envision students have had a meeting.

STUDENT CHECKPOINT ORGANIZER

EXAMPLE

Student Name: _Brendan_   Checkpoint Date: _September 18, 2XXX_

Party Type: _Summer Celebration_   Party Theme: _Eggs_

directions

Bring the following items to the Checkpoint Meeting:
- your Student Instruction Guide.
- your completed Student Checkpoint Organizer.
- all of your project materials.

questions

1. Do you have any questions about your project at this point?

   Will you read my bullet point reasons? Are they okay?

2. Is there any part of your project that you need help with?

   Not right now. I'm excited for my party!

3. Is there anything else about your project that you would like to talk about?

   May I cut balloons off of my organizer and make them 3-D?

4. Which requirement was your favorite to work on so far?

   I liked learning how to make bullet points on the computer.

TEACHER CHECKPOINT RECORD

EXAMPLE

student name	party type and theme	checkpoint 1 notes	checkpoint 2 notes	checkpoint 3 notes
1. Michael	First Lost Tooth Feast, Ice Cream	Great start! Neat and organized.		
2. Alysssa	Summer Celebration, Eggs	Finished all objectives to this point. Nice work.		
3. Brian	Nick's Birthday Party, Trains	Alex will assist Brian with bullet points. Check back.		
4. Alex	Graduating Second Grade Fiesta, Hats	Looks good! Needs paper for banner.		
5. Lauren	First Day of Winter Party, Chocolate	Creative and colorful! Needs a binder.		
6. Brendan	New Puppy Party, Bones	Fun ideas. Off to a great start.		
7. Ella	Reading Goal Celebration, Books	Excellent work so far!		
8. Teagan	Friendship Party, Movie Characters	Already adding extra ideas. Fantastic!		
9. Earl	Cousins' Day Shindig, Backwards	Finished all objectives to this point. Looks good!		
10.				

TEACHER INSTRUCTION GUIDE

STEP 5
Prepare for the Project Expo and the Classroom Presentations

> **IMPORTANT!**
> The expo is an extremely important part of the Envision experience. While it requires a certain amount of work, it solidifies the entire experience for you, your students and your students' parents. It is very important that students have a special opportunity to shine, and to display all of the hard work they have done over the quarter. It is also extremely rewarding for you, who will not only be proud of the student accomplishments, but will also receive a lot of parent feedback at this time.

Prepare for the Project Expo:

5.1 Copy one Student Expo Invitation and use your Teacher Planning Guide to complete the expo information. The invitation is included on your CD if you wish to print them in color.

5.2 For each Envision student, copy a completed expo invitation and fold it accordingly.

Invite Families to the Project Expo:

5.3 Give a Student Expo Invitation to each Envision student. Point out to the students that there is an Expo Invitation Response included with the invitation for each family to sign, detach and return.

5.4 Send the Student Expo Invitations home with the students to their families.

Prepare for the Project Expo (Continued):

5.5 As the expo responses are returned to you, record the information in the correct columns of the Teacher Forms Checklist.

5.6 Based on the Expo Invitation Responses, review whether any students will need special equipment, such as computers, televisions or DVD players. Reserve the equipment if necessary.

5.7 Based on the Expo Invitation Responses, find and reserve a large enough expo location (classroom, library, gymnasium or hallway) in which to host the expo. Be sure the location can accommodate any equipment required by the students.

5.8 Create a general plan for ordering, obtaining and serving refreshments (optional).

5.9 Copy a Student Certificate for each Envision student. Complete the certificates and set them aside for the Project Expo. The certificate is included on your CD if you wish to print them in color.

5.10 Copy a Student Name Sign for each Envision student. Complete each name sign and set it aside for the Project Expo. The name sign is included on your CD if you wish to print them in color.

5.11 Walk the route from the entrance of the Project Expo building to the entrance of the Project Expo location itself. Count the number of Left and Right Arrow Signs you will need to post along the way. Make enough copies of each and set them aside for the Project Expo.

TEACHER INSTRUCTION GUIDE

Prepare for Classroom Presentations and the Project Expo:

5.12 Copy a Teacher Assessment for each Envision student to use for Classroom Presentations.

5.13 Copy a Student Self-Assessment for each Envision student. Set them aside for Student Self-Assessment time.

> **IMPORTANT!**
> Be sure to keep the Student Self-Assessments separate from the Teacher Assessments. The main reason for this is so that students are assessing themselves without seeing the points you have already given. Students cannot complete their Self-Assessments prior to your Teacher Assessments because they need to wait until after they have given their Classroom Presentations.

5.14 Confirm your room and equipment reservations for the Project Expo.

5.15 Purchase any optional supplies or refreshments you will need for the Project Expo.

YOU'RE INVITED!

PLEASE JOIN US FOR OUR ENVISION PARTY PLAN EXPO!

Why? _To view students' Envision accomplishments_

Who? _All are welcome – family and friends_

Where? _Mind Vine Elementary Gymnasium_

When? _Wednesday, Nov. 7, 2XXX · 6:30 pm – 7:30 pm_

Remember to bring your camera!

EXPO INVITATION RESPONSE

Please fill out and return by: _Friday, Nov. 2_

Student Name: _____

Student Attending? ❏ Yes ❏ No

Number of Student Guests Attending: _____

Will your child need any special school equipment for the expo (i.e., computer or TV)? Please List: _____
_____

Thank you.
We look forward to seeing you at this special event!

EXAMPLE

CERTIFICATE OF ACHIEVEMENT

Michael

AWARDED TO

November 7, 2XXX

DATE

Mrs. Bondy

SIGNATURE

envision

PARTY PLAN PROJECT

Michael

STUDENT

envision

EXAMPLE

TEACHER ASSESSMENT

PARTY PLAN
100 total possible for the project.

Requirements	Possible Points	Teacher Points	Average Points
Week 1: Party Type (9 points)			
1. **Party Type Balloon Brainstorm:** Think about different events in life that you might like to celebrate. Using your Balloon Brainstorm organizer (attached), write various types of parties you might like to have to celebrate these events. Record one type of party on each balloon, using at least five of the balloons.	2		
2. **Party Type Balloon Color Ranking:** Choose three different colors of crayons, pencils or markers. Now choose one of those colors for your best ideas, a second color for your second choice ideas and a third color for your least favorite ideas. Color each balloon on your Balloon Brainstorm organizer according to your color key. Leave a small amount of white around the words in your balloons so they can be read. To help make your coloring decisions, think about why you might enjoy one party more than another.	3		
3. **Party Type Balloon Choice:** Read your best idea colored balloons and from those, choose the party idea that that you think would be the most exciting to plan. On your Balloon Brainstorm organizer, outline your party choice balloon with a new color that makes it stand out. This will be the party you plan for this project. Include your finished Balloon Brainstorm organizer as the first page in your portfolio.	1		
4. **Computer-Created Bullet Point Reasons:** Use the computer and title a new document, "I chose this party because…" Next, use bullet points to list at least four reasons your chose the party you did. You may also include reasons for not choosing your other party ideas. Include this as the second page in your portfoio.	3		
Week 2: Party Theme (15 points)			
1. **Theme Idea Labels:** Using your Theme Idea Labels organizer (attached), write five or more different themes that you might choose for your party. Record one theme idea on each label. Save these labels for the "Theme Choice Party Hat" step, below.	2		

STUDENT SELF-ASSESSMENT

PARTY PLAN
100 total possible for the project.

Requirements	Possible Points	Student Points
Week 1: Party Type (9 points)		
1. **Party Type Balloon Brainstorm:** Think about different events in life that you might like to celebrate. Using your Balloon Brainstorm organizer (attached), write various types of parties you might like to have to celebrate these events. Record one type of party on each balloon, using at least five of the balloons.	2	
2. **Party Type Balloon Color Ranking:** Choose three different colors of crayons, pencils or markers. Now choose one of those colors for your best ideas, a second color for your second choice ideas and a third color for your least favorite ideas. Color each balloon on your Balloon Brainstorm organizer according to your color key. Leave a small amount of white around the words in your balloons so they can be read. To help make your coloring decisions, think about why you might enjoy one party more than another.	3	
3. **Party Type Balloon Choice:** Read your best idea colored balloons and from those, choose the party idea that that you think would be the most exciting to plan. On your Balloon Brainstorm organizer, outline your party choice balloon with a new color that makes it stand out. This will be the party you plan for this project. Include your finished Balloon Brainstorm organizer as the first page in your portfolio.	1	
4. **Computer-Created Bullet Point Reasons:** Use the computer and title a new document, "I chose this party because…" Next, use bullet points to list at least four reasons your chose the party you did. You may also include reasons for not choosing your other party ideas. Include this as the second page in your portfoio.	3	
Week 2: Party Theme (15 points)		
1. **Theme Idea Labels:** Using your Theme Idea Labels organizer (attached), write five or more different themes that you might choose for your party. Record one theme idea on each label. Save these labels for the "Theme Choice Party Hat" step, below.	2	

Copyright © 2012 by Melanie L. Bondy, ENVISION: PARTY PLAN, Mind Vine Press, LLC. This page may not be photocopied or reproduced in any way.

TEACHER INSTRUCTION GUIDE

STEP 6
Conduct the Classroom Presentations

This is the first occasion for your Envision students to share their completed projects with an audience – in this case, you and the rest of the class. It is the only opportunity they will have to formally present their projects to an audience.

> **Note:** For logistics and classroom management reasons, choose the Option below that best describes your Envision student participation and follow its set of directions.

Classroom Presentations Option A:
A minority of the class is participating in Envision

6A.1 When students arrive at school on Classroom Presentation day, have them place their materials in a safe location.

6A.2 Just before you are ready to begin the presentations, gather a pen and the Teacher Assessments that you copied in Step 5.

> **Note:** This will be your only opportunity to assess the presentations. However, you will have more time later to assess the exhibits.

6A.3 Set a table in the front of the room.

6A.4 Ask all students to sit at their regular classroom seats and face the front of the room.

TEACHER INSTRUCTION GUIDE

6A.5 Sit in a location that will not be distracting to the presenter or the audience, yet will allow you to assess each presentation and each exhibit item clearly.

6A.6 The First Presenter: Ask for a volunteer or select a student to begin presenting. The student who will present should carry her portfolio and exhibit components to the front of the room and set them on the table. (Enlist another student to help if necessary.)

6A.7 Record the presenting student's name on a Teacher Assessment.

6A.8 Have the student stand to the side of her project and begin her presentation.

6A.9 Assess the student's presentation using a Teacher Assessment.

> **IMPORTANT!**
> This will be your only opportunity to assess the presentation.

6A.10 Use any extra time during the presentation to begin assessing the student's exhibit components.

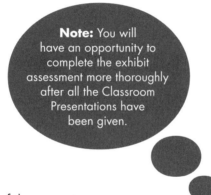

Note: You will have an opportunity to complete the exhibit assessment more thoroughly after all the Classroom Presentations have been given.

6A.11 Allow peers to ask questions of the presenter.

6A.12 Transitioning Between Presenters:
When the first presenter concludes her presentation and everyone has finished applauding, ask for the next volunteer or call the next student's name. As the next student is gathering his materials, the first student can remove hers and set them back where they had been placed earlier. Allow a minute or two for transitioning. Continue this process until all of your Envision students have presented.

6A.13 Conclude the presentations by thanking your Envision students for all of their hard work and by thanking all students for their attention.

Classroom Presentations Option B:
A majority or all of the class is participating in Envision

6B.1 When students arrive at school on Classroom Presentation day, have them place their materials in a safe location.

6B.2 Just before you are ready to begin the presentations, gather a pen, the Teacher Assessments (copied in Step 5) and a clipboard or other writing surface to carry with you.

TEACHER INSTRUCTION GUIDE

6B.3 Instruct all Envision students to set up their portfolios and exhibits at their desks. This should take just a few minutes.

6B.4 The First Presenter: Ask for a volunteer or select a student to begin presenting.

6B.5 Record the presenting student's name on an assessment, using your clipboard for writing support.

6B.6 Have the student remain at her seat and stand to the side of her project. Ask all other students to quietly gather in front of her.

6B.7 Stand in a location that will not be distracting to the presenter or the audience, yet will allow you to assess each presentation and each exhibit item clearly.

6B.8 Allow the student to begin her presentation.

6B.9 Assess the student's presentation using a Teacher Assessment.

> **IMPORTANT!**
> This will be your only opportunity to assess the presentation.

6B.10 Use any extra time during the presentation to begin assessing her exhibit components.

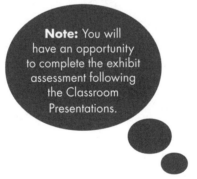

Note: You will have an opportunity to complete the exhibit assessment following the Classroom Presentations.

6B.11 Transitioning Between Presenters: When the first presenter concludes her presentation and everyone has finished applauding, ask for the next volunteer or call the next student's name. Direct everyone to quietly move to that student's exhibit. Continue this process until all of your Envision students have presented.

6B.12 Conclude the presentations by thanking your Envision students for all of their hard work and by thanking all students for their attention. Keep all projects set up as you will now be conducting the Classroom Expo.

TEACHER INSTRUCTION GUIDE

STEP 7
Classroom Expo & Student Self-Assessment

The Classroom Expo is a time where classroom peers have a chance to walk around and view the projects. Each Envision student will stand with his project and answer any questions that his peers may have. This will now be your opportunity to further assess the exhibit components. Again, for logistics and classroom management reasons, choose the option below that best describes your Envision student participation and follow its set of directions.

Classroom Expo and Student Self-Assessment
Option A: A minority of the class is participating in Envision

7A.1 Just before you are ready to begin the Classroom Expo, gather a pen, the Teacher Assessments (copied in Step 5) and a clipboard or other writing surface to carry with you.

7A.2 Direct your non-Envision students to remain seated at their desks.

7A.3 Have your Envision students quietly set up their portfolios and exhibits. This can be done at a single large table, on a counter space or at each student's desk.

7A.4 Have each Envision student stand beside her exhibit.

7A.5 Instruct the rest of the class to put away their work materials and begin visiting each Envision exhibit. Encourage them to ask questions about the projects. Tell them the approximate amount of time they will have to visit all the exhibits.

7A.6 While students are enjoying the Classroom Expo, walk around the room and assess each student's exhibit components using your clipboard, pen and Teacher Assessments.

> **IMPORTANT!**
> Students will be leaving their exhibits in the classroom until they set up for the Project Expo. Therefore, if you need more time to assess the exhibits, you may continue the assessments at another time prior to the expo.

7A.7 At the Classroom Expo conclusion, ask non-Envision students to return to their desks. Allow your Envision students a few minutes to take down their exhibits and return them to a safe location.

7A.8 Have Envision students return to their desks.

7A.9 Distribute the Student Self-Assessments (copied in Step 5) to Envision students. Have the students privately complete their points and point totals for each component. Instruct the students to hand them in to you when they are finished.

TEACHER INSTRUCTION GUIDE

Classroom Expo and Student Self-Assessment
Option B: A majority or all of the class is participating in Envision

7B.1 Continue to carry your clipboard, pen and Teacher Assessments to use during the Classroom Expo.

7B.2 Direct half of your Envision students to stand beside their exhibits.

7B.3 Instruct the rest of the class to begin visiting each Envision exhibit. Encourage them to ask questions about the projects. Tell them the approximate amount of time they will have to visit all the exhibits.

7B.4 While students are enjoying the Classroom Expo, walk around the room and assess the vacant student exhibits using your clipboard, pen and Teacher Assessments.

7B.5 When you are ready to move on to the second set of exhibits, direct your students to switch roles. Any non-Envision students can continue visiting exhibits they have not yet been to.

7B.6 Again, proceed with the Classroom Expo remembering to tell students the approximate amount of time they will have to visit the remaining exhibits.

7B.7 During this time, walk around the room and assess the remaining student exhibits.

> **IMPORTANT!**
> Students will be leaving their exhibits in the classroom until they set up for the Project Expo. Therefore, if you need more time to assess the exhibits, you may continue the assessments at another time prior to the expo.

7B.8 At the Classroom Expo conclusion, ask students to help one another take down their exhibits and return them to a safe location. Non-Envision students can help with this as well.

7B.9 Have all students return to their desks.

7B.10 Distribute the Student Self-Assessments (copied in Step 5) to Envision students. Have the students privately complete their points and point totals for each component. Instruct the students to hand them in to you when they are finished.

TEACHER INSTRUCTION GUIDE

STEP 8
Final Preparation for the Project Expo

Students take immense pride in sharing the fruits of their hard work with relatives and friends at the Project Expo. The expo offers a fun, festive environment where family and friends have the opportunity to meet all the Envision students and see their projects. It is also a forum for Envision students to share their project experiences and educational growth with guests.

Final Preparation for the Project Expo:

8.1 Ensure that tables, desks, chairs, refreshments and any special equipment are in place. Refer to your Teacher Forms Checklist for any special equipment needed.

8.2 Prepare and set aside a camera and video recorder, if desired, for your use at the expo.

8.3 Assign each student a location for exhibit setup.

8.4 Place the appropriate Student Name Sign (prepared in Step 5) at each student's exhibit area.

8.5 Allow small groups of students to take their project components to their designated exhibit areas.

8.6 Hang the Expo Arrow Signs (prepared in Step 5) along the route from the entrance of the building to the specific expo location itself.

8.7 Have the Student Certificates (prepared in Step 5) ready to present to the students at the expo.

8.8 Explain to students that they should be on their best behavior at the expo. Also explain that each student should remain at his or her exhibit for the majority of the expo to answer guests' project questions.

TEACHER INSTRUCTION GUIDE

STEP 9
The Project Expo:

9.1 Greet the students and guests as they enter the expo location. Ask students to go directly to their exhibits. Invite guests to explore and ask questions at each exhibit.

9.2 Be sure to take photos, and video if desired, of the expo. Obtain at least one photo of each student with his exhibit to post later on your project bulletin board. Also, the photos may come in handy if you need to double check anything during your final project assessment.

9.3 After guests have had time to view the projects, gather everyone together and formally present the Student Certificates to the Envision students. Thank everyone for attending and for supporting the hard work of the students. Ask the Envision students to take home all of their project components except for the portfolios. You will need to assess these, and you will return them with each student's final Teacher Assessment.

9.4 Collect the portfolios so that you can complete the Teacher Assessment for each project.

STEP 10
Conclusion, Teacher Assessment and Student Review
Conclusion and Teacher Assessment:

10.1 Print all expo photos.

10.2 Arrange the expo photos on a bulletin board. This will show the students your pride in their work.

10.3 Referring to student portfolios, complete the "Teacher Points" column for the "Component 1: Building Your Project Portfolio" section of the Teacher Assessments.

10.4 Add all columns on each Teacher Assessment, recording the "Total Points" for each component along with the "Total Project Points" at the end of the assessment.

10.5 Average the amount of each "Total Points" section from each student's Student Self-Assessment with the corresponding "Total Points" amount for each component section on his or her Teacher Assessment.

10.6 Record each component's average amount in the "Average Points" column of the Teacher Assessment for each student

10.7 For each student, record the "Total Project Points" in your personal record book. Staple each student's Student Self-Assessment to their Teacher Assessment. Copy these packets for your records.

Student Review:

10.8 Return each student's portfolio and completed assessment packet.

10.9 Allow the students time to review their assessment packets and ask questions if they wish.

> **IMPORTANT!**
> There is an optional Student Post Project Reflection at the end of Appendix 1. It encourages reflective writing and student goal setting for future projects.

CONGRATULATIONS ON PROJECT COMPLETION!

APPENDIX 1:
PARTY PLAN FORMS

PARTY PLAN AND BLOOM'S TAXONOMY

Levels From Lowest to Highest:
KNOWLEDGE • COMPREHENSION • APPLICATION • ANALYSIS • EVALUATION • SYNTHESIS
Below you will find each Party Plan requirement, along with its corresponding level of Bloom's Taxonomy.

> **IMPORTANT!**
> The levels listed above are cumulative. For example, the highest level of thinking, Synthesis, incorporates all other levels of thinking: Knowledge, Comprehension, Application, Analysis and Evaluation.

WEEK 1: PARTY TYPE
Total Possible Portfolio Points: 9 out of 100 total possible for the project.

1. **Party Type Balloon Brainstorm** (2 points): Think about different events in life that you might like to celebrate. Using your Balloon Brainstorm organizer (attached), write various types of parties you might like to have to celebrate these events. Record one type of party on each balloon, using at least five of the balloons. You will also use this organizer for the next step. **ANALYSIS**

2. **Party Type Balloon Color Ranking** (3 points): Choose three different colors of crayons, pencils or markers. Now choose one of those colors for your best ideas, a second color for your second choice ideas and a third color for your least favorite ideas. Record them on your Balloon Brainstorm organizer. Color each balloon on your Balloon Brainstorm organizer according to your color key. Leave a small amount of white around the words in your balloons so they can be read. To help make your coloring decisions, think about why you might enjoy one party more than another. You will also use this organizer for the next step. **EVALUATION**

3. **Party Type Balloon Choice** (1 point): Read your Best Idea colored balloons and from those, choose the party idea that you think would be the most exciting to plan. On your Balloon Brainstorm organizer, outline your party choice balloon with a new color that makes it stand out. This will be the party you plan for this project. Include your finished Balloon Brainstorm organizer as the first page in your portfolio. **EVALUATION**

4. **Computer-Created Bullet Point Reasons** (3 points): Use the computer and title a new document, "I chose this party because..." Next, use bullet points to list at least four reasons you chose the party you did. You may also include reasons for not choosing your other party ideas. Include this as the second page in your portfolio. **ANALYSIS**

WEEK 2: PARTY THEME
Total Possible Portfolio Points: 15 out of 100 total possible for the project.

1. **Theme Idea Labels** (2 points): Using your Theme Idea Labels organizer (attached), write five or more different themes that you might choose for your party. Follow the organizer directions to rank and record your idea labels. Save these labels for the "Theme Choice Party Hat" step, below. **ANALYSIS**

2. **Theme Choice Party Hat** (3 points): Cut out each of your Theme Idea Labels. Glue the labels onto the Theme Choice Party Hat organizer (attached) in order, so your favorite theme is in the party hat pompon and your least favorite theme idea is in the bottom stripe of the hat. Color your party hat leaving the labels white. The theme idea in your party hat's pompon will be the theme for your party. Cut out your finalized party hat and save it to attach to your final display board. You may also want to make a copy of your hat to include in your portfolio. **EVALUATION**

PARTY PLAN AND BLOOM'S TAXONOMY

3. **Theme Party Banner** (5 points): Design a banner that celebrates your party and party theme. Be sure to include the type of party it is. Write words and draw pictures that go along with your theme. Make it festive and be creative! Save your finished banner to use as part of your final exhibit. **SYNTHESIS**

4. **Theme Picture Book Choices** (5 points): Locate at least three fiction or non fiction picture books related to your theme. Using the Theme Picture Book Choices organizer, record the book titles and the name of each book's author. Read the books and choose your favorite. Record your favorite book choice and write at least three reasons why you think other people should read this book. Include this as the next page in your portfolio. **EVALUATION**

WEEK 3: PARTY DETAILS AND STRATEGIES
Total Possible Portfolio Points: 7 out of 100 total possible for the project.

1. **Party Planning Guide I** (3 points): Using the Party Planning Guide I organizer (attached), think about and research different options for the sections listed. For each section, make a decision and record it. Include your finished guide as the next page in your portfolio. **EVALUATION**

2. **Environmental Strategies** (4 points): Use the Environmental Strategies organizer (attached) to create ways of reducing, reusing and recycling at your party. Add your completed Environmental Strategies organizer as the next page in your portfolio. **SYNTHESIS**

WEEK 4: PARTY ACTIVITIES AND DETAILS
Total Possible Portfolio Points: 16 out of 100 total possible for the project.

1. **Party Game** (6 points): Invent a party game that relates to your theme. Complete the Party Game organizer (attached) and include its two pages as the next pages in your portfolio. **SYNTHESIS**

2. **Craft Creation and Model** (8 points): Design a craft your party guests can make and take home with them. Your craft should relate to your party theme. Save your craft model for part of your final project exhibit. Use the Craft Creation organizer (attached) to record your craft idea and directions. Include its two pages as the next pages in your portfolio. **SYNTHESIS**

3. **Party Planning Guide II** (2 points): Use the Party Planning Guide II organizer (attached) to think about different options for the party planning sections listed. For each section, make a decision and record it. Add this finished organizer as the next page in your portfolio. **EVALUATION**

WEEK 5: PARTY MAILINGS
Total Possible Portfolio Points: 9 out of 100 total possible for the project.

1. **Computer-Created Invitation** (5 points): Using the computer, design and write an invitation for your party. Be sure that the invitation design relates to your theme. Use both of your Party Planning Guides and make sure you include the starred information from them. Include a response date and contact information such as your phone number and email address. Don't use your real contact information! Instead, be creative and make up your contact information. Save your invitation for your final exhibit. You may also include an extra copy of it as the next page in your portfolio. **SYNTHESIS**

2. **Community Map** (4 points): Draw a map of your party's location including its surrounding area with roads and landmarks. Include a map key and a compass rose. Save this for your final display board. You may also include an extra copy of this as the next page in your portfolio. **SYNTHESIS**

PARTY PLAN AND BLOOM'S TAXONOMY

WEEK 6: PARTY FARE
Total Possible Portfolio Points: 14 out of 100 total possible for the project.

1. **Food and Drink Budget Poster** (6 points): At the top of a poster or large sheet of paper, record the title, "Party Food and Drink Choices." Below your title, record the number of party guests you will be inviting. Next, divide your poster into two equal sections, one labeled, "Food," and one labeled, "Drinks". Look through sale ads from grocery stores and choose five or six foods that you would enjoy serving at your party. Cut each food choice from the paper with its price. Arrange the pictures so they are equally spaced on the "Food" side of your poster. Using a party food budget of $15 total, calculate the cost to buy enough of each food item. Record the total cost with each item. Circle the food you will buy for your party, making sure it is within your food budget.

    Repeat this process using the other side of your poster for your party drinks. Your party drink budget is $10 total. Save the poster for your final display board. **SYNTHESIS**

2. **Serving Plan Chart** (4 points): Look over your snack and drink choices. Decide what types of serving supplies you will need. This includes items you need to serve and items your guests will need to enjoy your snacks and drinks. Create your own chart that shows the serving items needed, the number of each needed and each item's use. Include this as the next page in your portfolio. **SYNTHESIS**

3. **Serving Area Illustration** (4 points): Decide where you will serve your party snacks and drinks. Draw a picture of your serving area. Be sure to include your snacks, drinks and serving pieces. Label the items in your illustration. Be creative with color, photos, stickers, magazine clippings or other ideas. Save this for your final display board. You may also want to make a copy of your illustration to include in your portfolio. **SYNTHESIS**

WEEK 7: FINISHING TOUCHES
Total Possible Portfolio Points: 10 out of 100 total possible for the project.

1. **Sequence of Preparations and Events** (3 points): Use the two Sequence of Preparations and Events organizers (attached) to plan the order in which you will do things for and at your party. Include the completed Sequence of Preparations and Events II organizer as the next page in your portfolio. **SYNTHESIS**

2. **Weather Adjustments** (4 points): Research the average weather patterns for your party location at the time of year you will have your party. Using the Weather Adjustments organizer, record this information with the heading, "Weather Patterns." Be sure to write the source for where you found your information. Next, explain how you think these weather patterns might affect your party. Last, describe at least two party adjustments you may need to make due to weather that may occur. Include this organizer as the next page in your portfolio. **SYNTHESIS**

3. **Possible Accidents and Safety Precautions** (3 points): Research and think about different accidents that could happen at your party. Use the Possible Accidents and Safety Precautions organizer (attached) to list at least three possible accidents that may occur. Next, create and record at least two precaution ideas for each of these accidents. Include this organizer as the next page in your portfolio. **SYNTHESIS**

PARTY PLAN AND BLOOM'S TAXONOMY

WEEKS 8 AND 9: REMAINING PORTFOLIO MATERIALS AND EXHIBIT
Total Possible Portfolio Points: 12 out of 100 total possible for the project.

1. **Table of Contents** (2 points): Create a table of contents that lists all the pages of your portfolio along with their page numbers. **COMPREHENSION**

2. **Cover Page** (2 points): Create an eye-catching cover page for your portfolio that includes a creative title for your project as well as your name and the Classroom Presentation date. **SYNTHESIS**

3. **Portfolio** (2 points): Organize all of your materials into a three-ring binder. The table of contents should be first, followed by your project work from each week in the order presented. Your cover page should be on the front of your portfolio. **SYNTHESIS**

4. **Display Board** (3 points): Use a large two- or three-panel display board to showcase your project. It must include your project's title and your name. Remember to include your theme choice party hat, community map, food and drink budget poster and serving area illustration on your display board. You may then choose to add copies of any of your portfolio items or any additional materials that you wish. **SYNTHESIS**

5. **Exhibit** (3 points): Arrange your portfolio, theme banner, theme picture book choice, party craft model, computer-created invitation and any additional materials you wish to include in an appealing and informative way. **SYNTHESIS**

WEEK 10: CLASSROOM PRESENTATION
Total Possible Portfolio Points: 8 out of 100 total possible for the project.

1. **Your Presentation**

   - Party Type and Theme (1 point): Share your party type and theme. **KNOWLEDGE**

   - Game or Craft (2 points): Explain and show your game or craft. **COMPREHENSION**

   - Book Talk (5 points): Reread the book you chose as your favorite picture book choice. Choose a section from the book (two to three paragraphs) that would be enjoyable to share with others. Next, practice reading the paragraphs out loud until you can read them smoothly and clearly. **COMPREHENSION**

   For your presentation book talk:

   - Read the book's title and author. Show the cover of the book. **KNOWLEDGE**

   - Read aloud the section you chose and practiced. **COMPREHENSION**

   - Share your reasons that others should read this book. Remember that you already recorded reasons on your Theme Picture Book Choices organizer. **COMPREHENSION**

TEACHER COPY CHART

Step Number	Form Title	Number of Copies
1.1	Teacher Planning Guide	1 only
2.1–2.3	Parent Envision Introduction Letter	1 completed, then 1 per student
	Parent Party Plan Introduction Letter	1 completed, then 1 per student
	Student Party Plan Introduction Letter	1 completed only
	Student Instruction Guide	1 only
3.1–3.4	Teacher Forms Checklist	1 completed only
	Student Commitment Contract	1 completed, then 1 per student
3.5	Student Party Plan Introduction Letter*	1 completed, then one per student
	Each Week's Student Instruction Guide + Organizers*	1 per student
	Each Week's Resource Card Appendix Pages*	1 per student (optional)
4.1–4.2	Student Checkpoint Organizer	1 per student
	Teacher Checkpoint Record	1 completed only
5.1–5.2	Student Expo Invitation	1 completed, then one per student
5.9–5.11	Student Certificate	1 per student, then each completed
	Student Name Sign (optional)	1 per student, then each completed
	Left Arrow Sign	Amount needed
	Right Arrow Sign	Amount needed
5.12–5.13	Teacher Assessment	1 per student
	Student Self-Assessment	1 per student

*Staple these items into a packet for each student.

TEACHER PLANNING GUIDE

Week	Event (Step Numbers)	Day and Date	Time
1	Plan and Prepare for the Project (1.1–1.2)		
	Prepare for Party Plan Introduction (2.1–2.3)		
	Party Plan Introduction (2.4–2.7)		
	Prepare for Party Plan Implementation (3.1–3.6)		
	Party Plan Implementation (3.7–3.16)		
2	Distribute this week's section of the Student Instruction Guide (SIG) and its corresponding Organizers.		
3	Prepare for the Checkpoint Meetings (4.1–4.2)		
	Distribute SIG and Organizers, then Checkpoint Organizers (4.3-4.6)		
	Checkpoint Meetings (4.7–4.12)		
4	Distribute this week's section of the Student Instruction Guide (SIG) and its corresponding Organizers.		
5	Prepare for the Checkpoint Meetings (4.1–4.2)		
	Distribute SIG and Organizers, then Checkpoint Organizers (4.3-4.6)		
	Checkpoint Meetings (4.7–4.12)		
6	Distribute this week's section of the Student Instruction Guide (SIG) and its corresponding Organizers.		
7	Prepare for the Checkpoint Meetings (4.1–4.2)		
	Distribute SIG and Organizers, then Checkpoint Organizers (4.3-4.6)		
	Checkpoint Meetings (4.7–4.12)		
8	Prepare for the Party Plan Expo (5.1–5.2)		
	Distribute SIG and Organizers, and Invite Families to the Party Plan Expo (5.3–5.4)		
	Prepare for the Party Plan Expo Ctd. (5.5–5.11)		
9	Prepare for Classroom Presentations and the Party Plan Expo (5.12–5.15)		
	Classroom Presentations (6A.1–6A.13 or 6B.1–6B.12)		
	Classroom Expo and Student Self-Assessment (7A.1–7A.9 or 7B.1–7B.10)		
10	Final Preparation for the Party Plan Expo (8.1–8.8)		
	Party Plan Expo (9.1–9.4)		
	Conclusion and Teacher Assessment (10.1–10.7)		
	Student Review (10.8–10.9)		

*Events scheduled with the class are in black.

 introduction letter

Dear Parent(s),

I am happy to inform you that your child has been invited to participate in an advanced academic program called Envision. I am sending you this letter to explain the program and ask for your permission to include your child in this special opportunity.

Envision is an exciting program designed for students who are not sufficiently challenged by the standard grade-level curriculum. The focus of the program is on developing high-level critical thinking and creativity. It guides students through real-world-based projects that encourage them to envision how they might achieve their personal goals in the future.

Your child is being invited to participate in the Party Plan project, which allows students to plan a themed party to celebrate a special event.

Students will work on Envision during class time, free time and at home.

To give permission for your child to participate in Envision, simply sign the Envision Permission Form at the bottom of this letter, detach it and return the form to me. If you want your child to participate in Envision, please read the attached Parent Party Plan Introduction Letter. The letter introduces you to the project, informs you of important dates and requests permission for your child's continued participation.

Envision promises to be a wonderful learning opportunity for your child. I look forward to hearing from you. Please feel free to contact me if you have any questions.

Sincerely,

_____

_____

- -

 permission form

Please fill out this section, detach and return as soon as possible.   Date: _____

❏ I have read the Parent Envision Introduction Letter and give my child permission to participate in the Envision program.

❏ I have read the Parent Envision Introduction Letter and do not give my child permission to participate in the Envision program.

Child's Name: _____   Parent's Signature: _____

parent party plan introduction letter

Dear Parent(s),

Welcome to Party Plan, a project from the Envision program that will challenge and inspire your child. Party Plan will immediately engage your child as its challenge is to plan a themed party to celebrate a special event.

For this project, your child will choose an event to celebrate and a theme to incorporate into his or her party. Next, your child will create a party banner and read books related to the party theme. Your child will also create a party game, craft, invitation, map, food and drink budget poster, serving area illustration and much more. Most of these materials will be collected in a portfolio. Next, your child will design and create an exhibit that captures and conveys the highlights of his or her Party Plan project. Last, your child will present his or her project to the class.

A weekly Student Instruction Guide will be provided to guide your child, step by step, through this process. The Instruction Guide is a comprehensive list of project requirements and is designed to engage higher-level thinking. Along with this guide, your child will receive project organizers that correspond with certain objective requirements. The guide also references helpful resource cards that provide additional explanations, ideas, tips and directions. There will be a set of these cards to which your child may refer in our classroom.

Party Plan is designed to be worked on independently during class time, free time and at home. By scheduling several Checkpoint Meeting dates throughout the project, I will be able to monitor each student's progress. On these dates, I will meet with each student to discuss accomplishments and plan goals for the next checkpoint. I will also address any difficulties students might be having.

Party Plan will conclude with a celebratory Project Expo. The expo will be your child's opportunity to share his or her finished project with family, friends and other guests. Closer to the Project Expo date, you will receive a detailed invitation.

Dates to Remember:

Checkpoint 1: _____

Checkpoint 2: _____

Checkpoint 3: _____

Classroom Presentation: _____

Party Plan Expo: _____ , _____

Sincerely,

_____

student party plan introduction letter

Dear Student,

Welcome to Party Plan! This project will guide you to plan a party that celebrates an event of your choice.

Party Plan begins with choosing an event to and a party theme. You will also create a party banner, party game, craft, invitation, map, poster and much more.

You will store your Party Plan materials in a portfolio as you complete them. You will also build a display and share your project in class. At the end of the project, there will be a Project Expo. This is an event that will celebrate your hard work with family and friends.

You will work on Party Plan at school, during your free time and at home. Mostly, you will be expected to work on your own. We will have Checkpoint Meetings to discuss how your project is coming along and to provide help if needed. Between the checkpoints, you may talk about your project with other Envision students.

The attached Student Instruction Guide contains the first week's requirements for your Party Plan Project. The attached organizers will help you complete some of the requirements. There are also resource cards in our classroom that will help you complete your project successfully.

Dates to Remember:

Checkpoint 1: _____

Checkpoint 2: _____

Checkpoint 3: _____

Classroom Presentation: _____

Party Plan Expo: _____, _____

You are now ready to begin creating your Party Plan. Good luck and have fun!

Sincerely,

_____

_____

STUDENT INSTRUCTION GUIDE

Resource cards are available when you see a Party Plan icon 🎉. Party Plan Resource cards give you helpful information and examples. Also be sure to visit www.mindvinepress.com, other trustworthy Internet sites and library materials for more help.

WEEK 1: Party Type
Total Possible Points: 9 out of 100 total possible for the project.

1. 🎉 **Party Type Balloon Brainstorm** (2 points): Think about different events in life that you might like to celebrate. Using your Balloon Brainstorm organizer (attached), write various types of parties you might like to have to celebrate these events. Record one type of party on each balloon, using at least five of the balloons. You will also use this organizer for the next step.

2. **Party Type Balloon Color Ranking** (3 points): Choose three different colors of crayons, pencils or markers. Now choose one of those colors for your best ideas, a second color for your second choice ideas and a third color for your least favorite ideas. Record them on your Balloon Brainstorm organizer. Color each balloon on your Balloon Brainstorm organizer according to your color key. Leave a small amount of white around the words in your balloons so they can be read. To help make your coloring decisions, think about why you might enjoy one party more than another. You will also use this organizer for the next step.

3. **Party Type Balloon Choice** (1 point): Read your Best Idea colored balloons and from those, choose the party idea that you think would be the most exciting to plan. On your Balloon Brainstorm organizer, outline your party choice balloon with a new color that makes it stand out. This will be the party you plan for this project. Include your finished Balloon Brainstorm organizer as the first page in your portfolio.

4. 🎉 **Computer-Created Bullet Point Reasons** (3 points): Use the computer and title a new document, "I chose this party because..." Next, use bullet points to list at least four reasons you chose the party you did. You may also include reasons for not choosing your other party ideas. Include this as the second page in your portfolio.

BALLOON BRAINSTORM

Student Name: _____

directions

Read the Party Type Balloon Brainstorm student resource card. Think about some events in your life that you might like to celebrate. Write different types of parties you might like to have to celebrate these events. Record one type of party on each balloon, using at least five of the balloons. You will also use this organizer for the next step.

Color Key

Color for Best Ideas: _____

Color for Second Choice Ideas: _____

Color for Least Favorite Ideas: _____

STUDENT INSTRUCTION GUIDE

WEEK 2: Party Theme
Total Possible Points: 15 out of 100 total possible for the project.

1. **Theme Idea Labels** (2 points): Using your Theme Idea Labels organizer (attached), write five or more different themes that you might choose for your party. Follow the organizer directions to rank and record your idea labels. Save these labels for the "Theme Choice Party Hat" step, below.

2. **Theme Choice Party Hat** (3 points): Cut out each of your Theme Idea Labels. Read each label and think about which theme would be the best for your party. Glue the labels onto the Theme Choice Party Hat organizer (attached) in order, so your favorite theme is in the party hat pompon and your least favorite theme idea is in the bottom stripe of the hat. Color your party hat leaving the labels white. The theme idea in your party hat's pompon will be the theme for your party. Cut out your finalized party hat and save it to attach to your final display board. You may also want to make a copy of your hat to include in your portfolio.

3. **Theme Party Banner** (5 points): Design a banner that celebrates your party and party theme. Be sure to include the type of party it is. Write words and draw pictures that go along with your theme. Make it festive and be creative! Save your finished banner to use as part of your final exhibit.

4. **Theme Picture Book Choices** (5 points): Locate at least three fiction or non fiction picture books related to your theme. Using the Theme Picture Book Choices organizer, record the book titles and the name of each book's author. Read the books and choose your favorite. Record your favorite book choice and write at least three reasons why you think other people should read this book. Include this as the next page in your portfolio.

THEME IDEA LABELS

Student Name: _____

directions

Read the Theme Idea Labels student resource card. On the lines below, write five or more different themes that you might choose for your party. Choose and circle your top four theme ideas. Write your least favorite circled theme idea onto the number 4 dotted pattern. Write your next least favorite circled ideas on the numbers 2 and 3 dotted patterns. Write your favorite circled theme idea on the number 1 dotted pattern.

1.

2.

3.

4.

_____

_____

_____

_____

_____

_____

THEME CHOICE PARTY HAT

Student Name: _____

directions

Cut out each of the dotted theme idea labels from your Theme Ideas Labels organizer. Glue the labels onto the correctly numbered sections of this Theme Choice Party Hat. Your favorite theme will be on the pompon and your least favorite theme will be at the bottom of the hat. Color your party hat leaving the area around your words white. The theme idea in your party hat's pompon will be the theme for your party. Cut out your colored party hat and save it to attach to your final display board. You may also want to make a copy of your hat to include in your portfolio.

1. FAVORITE THEME
2. LABEL GOES HERE
3. LABEL GOES HERE
4. LABEL GOES HERE

THEME PICTURE BOOK CHOICES

Student Name: _____

my theme picture book information

TITLE	AUTHOR

my favorite theme picture book

Title: _____

Author: _____

personal evaluation

Reasons I think other people should read this book:

1. _____

2. _____

3. _____

STUDENT INSTRUCTION GUIDE

WEEK 3: PARTY DETAILS AND STRATEGIES
Total Possible Points: 7 out of 100 total possible for the project.

1. **Party Planning Guide I** (3 points): Using the Party Planning Guide I organizer (attached), think about and research different options for the sections listed. For each section, make a decision and record it. Include your finished guide as the next page in your portfolio.

2. **Environmental Strategies** (4 points): Use the Environmental Strategies organizer (attached) to create ways of reducing, reusing and recycling at your party. Add your completed Environmental Strategies organizer as the next page in your portfolio.

PARTY PLANNING GUIDE 1

Student Name: _____

type of party and theme

*Party Type: _____ *Party Theme: _____

location

*Where will you have your party? You may choose your house, a local park or a community location. _____

Will your party take place indoors, outdoors or both? _____

*What is the address of where you will have your party? If the location is your house, please invent an address; do not use your real address:
_____
_____

Who should you ask permission from to use this location? _____

guests

How many people will you invite to your party? Think about how much space you will have at your party location.
_____

Will your party include friends, family or both? Do not list specific names of party guests. _____

*Are there any special items your guests should bring? For example, do they need to bring a swimsuit and towel or wear a costume?
_____

*The starred items will be used later when writing your party invitation.

ENVIRONMENTAL STRATEGIES

Student Name: _____

directions

Read the Environmental Strategies student resource card for definitions and pictures of reducing, reusing and recycling. Complete the sections below.

illustrate and label

At least one way you will reduce waste at your party:

At least one way you will reuse at your party:

At least one way you will recycle at your party:

STUDENT INSTRUCTION GUIDE

WEEK 4: PARTY ACTIVITIES AND DETAILS
Total Possible Points: 16 out of 100 total possible for the project.

1. **Party Game** (6 points): Invent a party game that relates to your theme. Complete the Party Game organizer (attached) and include its two pages as the next pages in your portfolio.

2. **Craft Creation and Model** (8 points): Design a craft your party guests can make and take home with them. Your craft should relate to your party theme. Save your craft model for part of your final project exhibit. Use the Craft Creation organizer (attached) to record your craft idea and directions. Include its two pages as the next pages in your portfolio.

3. **Party Planning Guide II** (2 points): Use the Party Planning Guide II organizer (attached) to think about different options for the party planning sections listed. For each section, make a decision and record it. Add this finished organizer as the next page in your portfolio.

PARTY GAME

Student Name: _____

directions

Read the Party Game student resource card then complete the sections below.

about my game

Object of the game: _____
_____

How to set up: _____
_____
_____
_____

How to play: _____
_____
_____
_____
_____

Special rules:
1. _____
2. _____
3. _____
4. _____
5. _____

PARTY GAME CONTINUED

Student Name: _____

supplies needed

Item name	Number needed	Where it can be found

game prize

Create an illustration of a game prize your guests may win:

CRAFT CREATION

Student Name: _____

craft name

What is the name of the craft you are making? _____

directions

Read the Party Game student resource card then write detailed instructions for making your craft. Give measurements when needed:

1. _____
_____
2. _____
_____
3. _____
_____
4. _____
_____
5. _____
_____
6. _____
_____
7. _____
_____
8. _____
_____
9. _____
_____
10. _____
_____

CRAFT CREATION CONTINUED

Student Name: _____

supplies needed

Item name	Number needed	Where it can be found

photo or illustration

Take a photo or create an illustration of your craft model and add it here:

PARTY PLANNING GUIDE II

Student Name: _____

party date and times

*What day of the week will you have your party? Consider when your guests will likely be available. _____

*What month of the year will you have your party? Consider the activities you are planning. _____

*What times of day will you start and finish your party? Remember to write a.m. or p.m. with your times.

Start time: _____

Finish time: _____

*The starred items will be used later when writing your party invitation.

STUDENT INSTRUCTION GUIDE

WEEK 5: PARTY MAILINGS
Total Possible Points: 9 out of 100 total possible for the project.

1. **Computer-Created Invitation** (5 points): Using the computer, design and write an invitation for your party. Be sure that the invitation design relates to your theme. Use both of your Party Planning Guides and make sure you include the starred information from them. Include a response date and contact information such as your phone number and email address. Don't use your real contact information! Instead, be creative and make up your contact information. Save your invitation for your final exhibit. You may also include an extra copy of it as the next page in your portfolio.

2. **Community Map** (4 points): Draw a map of your party's location including its surrounding area with roads and landmarks. Include a map key and a compass rose. Save this for your final display board. You may also include an extra copy of this as the next page in your portfolio.

STUDENT INSTRUCTION GUIDE

WEEK 6: PARTY FARE
Total Possible Points: 14 out of 100 total possible for the project.

1. **Food and Drink Budget Poster** (6 points): At the top of a poster or large sheet of paper, record the title, "Party Food and Drink Choices." Below your title, record the number of party guests you will be inviting. Next, divide your poster into two equal sections, one labeled, "Food," and one labeled, "Drinks". Look through sale ads from grocery stores and choose five or six foods that you would enjoy serving at your party. Cut each food choice from the paper with its price. Arrange the pictures so they are equally spaced on the "Food" side of your poster. Using a party food budget of $15 total, calculate the cost to buy enough of each food item. Record the total cost with each item. Circle the food you will buy for your party, making sure it is within your food budget.

   Repeat this process using the other side of your poster for your party drinks. Your party drink budget is $10 total. Save the poster for your final display board.

2. **Serving Plan Chart** (4 points): Look over your snack and drink choices. Decide what types of serving supplies you will need. This includes items you need to serve and items your guests will need to enjoy your snacks and drinks. Create your own chart that shows the serving items needed, the number of each needed and each item's use. Include this as the next page in your portfolio.

3. **Serving Area Illustration** (4 points): Decide where you will serve your party snacks and drinks. Draw a picture of your serving area. Be sure to include your snacks, drinks and serving pieces. Label the items in your illustration. Be creative with color, photos, stickers, magazine clippings or other ideas. Save this for your final display board. You may also want to make a copy of your illustration to include in your portfolio.

STUDENT INSTRUCTION GUIDE

WEEK 7: FINISHING TOUCHES
Total Possible Points: 10 out of 100 total possible for the project.

1. **Sequence of Preparations and Events** (3 points): Use the two Sequence of Preparations and Events organizers (attached) to plan the order in which you will do things for and at your party. Include the completed Sequence of Preparations and Events II organizer as the next page in your portfolio.

2. **Weather Adjustments** (4 points): Research the average weather patterns for your party location at the time of year you will have your party. Using the Weather Adjustments organizer, record this information with the heading, "Weather Patterns." Be sure to write the source for where you found your information. Next, explain how you think these weather patterns might affect your party. Last, describe at least two party adjustments you may need to make due to weather that may occur. Include this organizer as the next page in your portfolio.

3. **Possible Accidents and Safety Precautions** (3 points): Research and think about different accidents that might happen at your party. Use the Possible Accidents and Safety Precautions organizer (attached) to list at least three possible accidents that may occur. Next, create and record at least two precaution ideas for each of these accidents. Include this organizer as the next page in your portfolio.

SEQUENCE OF PREPARATIONS AND EVENTS 1

Student Name: _____

directions

Read the Party Preparations Labels and Party Events Labels listed below. These are some of the main things you will need to do for and at your party. Next, read through your party plans making sure all preparations and events are listed below. Add additional preparations or events on the blank label lines if needed. You will continue this activity with the next organizer page.

Party Preparations Labels

- prepare food
- set up game
- set up serving area
- clean-up
- set up craft area
- decorate

_____
_____
_____
_____
_____
_____
_____

Party Events Labels

- introduce guests to each other
- play party game
- say good-bye and thank-you to guests
- greet guests
- serve food
- make craft

_____
_____
_____
_____
_____
_____
_____

SEQUENCE OF PREPARATIONS AND EVENTS II

Student Name: _____

directions

Cut out the Party Preparation Labels from organizer I. Arrange the labels until they are in the order of which will be done first, second and so forth. Rewrite each label in order onto its own line below. Repeat this process for the Party Events Labels. You may not use all of the lines below.

Party Preparations

1. _____
2. _____
3. _____
4. _____
5. _____
6. _____
7. _____
8. _____
9. _____
10. _____

Party Events

1. _____
2. _____
3. _____
4. _____
5. _____
6. _____
7. _____
8. _____
9. _____
10. _____

WEATHER ADJUSTMENTS

Student Name: _____

directions

Research the average weather patterns for your party location at the time of year you will have your party. Record this information below. Be sure to write the source for where you found your information. Next, explain how you think these weather patterns might affect your party. Last, describe at least two party adjustments you may need to make due to weather that may occur.

Weather Patterns: _____
_____
_____

Weather Pattern Information Source: _____
_____

How these weather patterns might affect my party: _____
_____
_____
_____

Party adjustments I may need to make due to weather that may occur:
1. _____
2. _____
3. _____

POSSIBLE ACCIDENTS AND SAFETY PRECAUTIONS

Student Name: _____

directions

Research and think about different accidents that could happen at your party. On the bold lines below, list at least three possible accidents that may occur. Next, create and record at least two safety precaution ideas for each of these possible accidents. Include your precautions on the lines below each possible accident. Note: A safety precaution is something you do ahead of time to prevent an accident.

Accident that could occur at my party: _____

Safety precaution idea: _____
_____

Safety precaution idea: _____
_____

Accident that could occur at my party: _____

Safety precaution idea: _____
_____

Safety precaution idea: _____
_____

Accident that could occur at my party: _____

Safety precaution idea: _____
_____

Safety precaution idea: _____
_____

STUDENT INSTRUCTION GUIDE

WEEKS 8 AND 9:
REMAINING PORTFOLIO MATERIALS AND EXHIBIT

Total Possible Points: 12 out of 100 total possible for the project.

1. **Table of Contents** (2 points): Create a table of contents that lists all the pages of your portfolio along with their page numbers.

2. **Cover Page** (2 points): Create an eye-catching cover page for your portfolio that includes a creative title for your project as well as your name and the Classroom Presentation date.

3. **Portfolio** (2 points): Organize all of your materials into a three-ring binder. The table of contents should be first, followed by your project work from each week in the order presented. Your cover page should be on the front of your portfolio.

4. **Display Board** (3 points): Use a large two- or three-panel display board to showcase your project. It must include your project's title and your name. Remember to include your theme choice party hat, community map, food and drink budget poster and serving area illustration on your display board. You may then choose to add copies of any of your portfolio items or any additional materials that you wish.

5. **Exhibit** (3 points): Arrange your portfolio, theme banner, theme picture book choice, party craft model, computer-created invitation and any additional materials you wish to include in an appealing and informative way.

STUDENT INSTRUCTION GUIDE

WEEK 10: CLASSROOM PRESENTATION

Total Possible Points: 8 out of 100 total possible for the project.

1. **Your Presentation**
   - Party Type and Theme (1 point): Share your party type and theme.
   - Game or Craft (2 points): Explain and show your game or craft.
   - Book Talk (5 points): Reread the book you chose as your favorite picture book choice. Choose a section from the book (two to three paragraphs) that would be enjoyable to share with others. Next, practice reading the paragraphs out loud until you can read them smoothly and clearly.

   For your presentation book talk:
   - Read the book's title and author. Show the cover of the book.
   - Read aloud the section you chose and practiced.
   - Share your reasons that others should read this book. Remember that you already recorded reasons on your Theme Picture Book Choices organizer.

TEACHER FORMS CHECKLIST

use this checklist to record forms submitted by the students

student name	envision permission form	student commitment contract	student checkpoint organizer 1	student checkpoint organizer 2	student checkpoint organizer 3	expo invitation response number attending special equip. needed
1.						
2.						
3.						
4.						
5.						
6.						
7.						
8.						
9.						
10.						
11.						
12.						
13.						
14.						
15.						
16.						
17.						
18.						
19.						
20.						
21.						
22.						
23.						
24.						
25.						

STUDENT COMMITMENT CONTRACT

expectations

project work time
I agree to:
- be responsible for following my Student Instruction Guide to do my work.
- keep track of all my project materials.
- work hard on Envision without disturbing others.
- save my unanswered questions until my teacher is free to talk.

checkpoint meetings
I will come prepared with:
- my Student Instruction Guide.
- my completed Student Checkpoint Organizer.
- all of my project materials.

important dates and times

Checkpoint 1: _____

Checkpoint 2: _____

Checkpoint 3: _____

Classroom Presentation: _____

Party Plan Expo: _____

_____

signatures

I agree to:
- meet expectations on the dates listed above.
- complete each of the project requirements to the best of my ability.
- bring my project work to school each day so that I can work on it during extra time.
- take my project work from school each night so that I can work on it at home.

I understand that this Envision project is a special opportunity, and that if I do not meet the above expectations, I may be asked to return to regular classroom activities.

Student Signature: _____ Date: _____

Parent Signature: _____ Date: _____

Please return this contract by: _____

STUDENT CHECKPOINT ORGANIZER

Student Name: _____ Checkpoint Date: _____

Party Type: _____ Party Theme: _____

directions

Bring the following items to the Checkpoint Meeting:
- your Student Instruction Guide.
- your completed Student Checkpoint Organizer.
- all of your project materials.

questions

1. Do you have any questions about your project at this point?
   _____
   _____

2. Is there any part of your project that you need help with?
   _____
   _____

3. Is there anything else about your project that you would like to talk about?
   _____
   _____

4. Which requirement was your favorite to work on so far?
   _____
   _____

TEACHER CHECKPOINT RECORD

student name	party type and theme	checkpoint 1 notes	checkpoint 2 notes	checkpoint 3 notes
1.				
2.				
3.				
4.				
5.				
6.				
7.				
8.				
9.				
10.				

YOU'RE INVITED!

EXPO INVITATION RESPONSE

Please fill out and return by: _____

Student name: _____

Student attending? ☐ Yes ☐ No

Number of student guests attending: _____

Will your child need any special school equipment for the expo (i.e., computer or TV)? Please List: _____

_____

Thank you.
We look forward to seeing you at this special event!

PLEASE JOIN US FOR OUR ENVISION PARTY PLAN EXPO!

Why? _____

Who? _____

Where? _____

When? _____

Remember to bring your camera!

CERTIFICATE OF ACHIEVEMENT

AWARDED TO

_____

DATE

_____

SIGNATURE

_____

envision®

PARTY PLAN PROJECT

STUDENT

envision

TEACHER ASSESSMENT

PARTY PLAN
100 total possible for the project.

Requirements	Possible Points	Teacher Points	Average Points
Week 1: Party Type (9 points)			
1. Party Type Balloon Brainstorm: Think about different events in life that you might like to celebrate. Using your Balloon Brainstorm organizer (attached), write various types of parties you might like to have to celebrate these events. Record one type of party on each balloon, using at least five of the balloons.	2		
2. Party Type Balloon Color Ranking: Choose three different colors of crayons, pencils or markers. Now choose one of those colors for your best ideas, a second color for your second choice ideas and a third color for your least favorite ideas. Record them on your Balloon Brainstorm organizer. Color each balloon on your Balloon Brainstorm organizer according to your color key. Leave a small amount of white around the words in your balloons so they can be read. To help make your coloring decisions, think about why you might enjoy one party more than another.	3		
3. Party Type Balloon Choice: Read your Best Idea colored balloons and from those, choose the party idea that you think would be the most exciting to plan. On your Balloon Brainstorm organizer, outline your party choice balloon with a new color that makes it stand out. This will be the party you plan for this project. Include your finished Balloon Brainstorm organizer as the first page in your portfolio.	1		
4. Computer-Created Bullet Point Reasons: Use the computer and title a new document, "I chose this party because..." Next, use bullet points to list at least four reasons you chose the party you did. You may also include reasons for not choosing your other party ideas. Include this as the second page in your portfolio.	3		
Week 2: Party Theme (15 points)			
1. Theme Idea Labels: Using your Theme Idea Labels organizer (attached), write five or more different themes that you might choose for your party. Follow the organizer directions to rank and record your idea labels. Save these labels for the "Theme Choice Party Hat" step, below.	2		
2. Theme Choice Party Hat: Cut out each of your Theme Idea Labels. Glue the labels onto the Theme Choice Party Hat organizer (attached) in order, so your favorite theme is in the party hat pompon and your least favorite theme idea is in the bottom stripe of the hat. Color your party hat leaving the labels white. The theme idea in your party hat's pompon will be the theme for your party. Cut out your finalized party hat and save it to attach to your final display board. You may also want to make a copy of your hat to include in your portfolio.	3		

TEACHER ASSESSMENT

3. Theme Party Banner: Design a banner that celebrates your party and party theme. Be sure to include the type of party it is. Write words and draw pictures that go along with your theme. Make it festive and be creative! Save your finished banner to use as part of your final exhibit.	5		
4. Theme Picture Book Choices: Locate at least three fiction or non fiction picture books related to your theme. Using the Theme Picture Book Choices organizer, record the book titles and the name of each book's author. Read the books and choose your favorite. Record your favorite book choice and write at least three reasons why you think other people should read this book. Include this as the next page in your portfolio.	5		
Week 3: Party Details and Strategies (7 points)			
1. Party Planning Guide I: Using the Party Planning Guide I organizer (attached), think about and research different options for the sections listed. For each section, make a decision and record it. Include your finished guide as the next page in your portfolio.	3		
2. Environmental Strategies: Use the Environmental Strategies organizer (attached) to create ways of reducing, reusing and recycling at your party. Add your completed Environmental Strategies organizer as the next page in your portfolio.	4		
Week 4: Party Activities and Details (16 points)			
1. Party Game: Invent a party game that relates to your theme. Complete the Party Game organizer (attached) and include its two pages as the next pages in your portfolio.	6		
2. Craft Creation and Model: Design a craft your party guests can make and take home with them. Your craft should relate to your party theme. Save your craft model for part of your final project exhibit. Use the Craft Creation organizer (attached) to record your craft idea and directions. Include its two pages as the next pages in your portfolio.	8		
3. Party Planning Guide II: Use the Party Planning Guide II organizer (attached) to think about different options for the party planning sections listed. For each section, make a decision and record it. Add this finished organizer as the next page in your portfolio.	2		

TEACHER ASSESSMENT

Week 5: Party Mailings (9 points)

1. Computer-Created Invitation: Using the computer, design and write an invitation for your party. Be sure that the invitation design relates to your theme. Use both of your Party Planning Guides and make sure you include the starred information from them. Include a response date and contact information such as your phone number and email address. Don't use your real contact information! Instead, be creative and make up your contact information. Save your invitation for your final exhibit. You may also include an extra copy of it as the next page in your portfolio.	5		
2. Community Map: Draw a map of your party's location including its surrounding area with roads and landmarks. Include a map key and a compass rose. Save this for your final display board. You may also include an extra copy of this as the next page in your portfolio.	4		

Week 6: Party Fare (14 points)

1. Food and Drink Budget Poster: At the top of a poster or large sheet of paper, record the title, "Party Food and Drink Choices." Below your title, record the number of party guests you will be inviting. Next, divide your poster into two equal sections, one labeled, "Food," and one labeled, "Drinks". Look through sale ads from grocery stores and choose five or six foods that you would enjoy serving at your party. Cut each food choice from the paper with its price. Arrange the pictures so they are equally spaced on the "Food" side of your poster. Using a party food budget of $15 total, calculate the cost to buy enough of each food item. Record the total cost with each item. Circle the food you will buy for your party, making sure it is within your food budget. Repeat this process using the other side of your poster for your party drinks. Your party drink budget is $10 total. Save the poster for your final display board.	6		
2. Serving Plan Chart: Look over your snack and drink choices. Decide what types of serving supplies you will need. This includes items you need to serve and items your guests will need to enjoy your snacks and drinks. Create your own chart that shows the serving items needed, the number of each needed and each item's use. Include this as the next page in your portfolio.	4		
3. Serving Area Illustration: Decide where you will serve your party snacks and drinks. Draw a picture of your serving area. Be sure to include your snacks, drinks and serving pieces. Label the items in your illustration. Be creative with color, photos, stickers, magazine clippings or other ideas. Save this for your final display board. You may also want to make a copy of your illustration to include in your portfolio.	4		

TEACHER ASSESSMENT

Week 7: Finishing Touches (10 points)

1. **Sequence of Preparations and Events:** Use the two Sequence of Preparations and Events organizers (attached) to plan the order in which you will do things for and at your party. Include the completed Sequence of Preparations and Events II organizer as the next page in your portfolio. | 3 | | |

2. **Weather Adjustments:** Research the average weather patterns for your party location at the time of year you will have your party. Using the Weather Adjustments organizer, record this information with the heading, "Weather Patterns." Be sure to write the source for where you found your information. Next, explain how you think these weather patterns might affect your party. Last, describe at least two party adjustments you may need to make due to weather that may occur. Include this organizer as the next page in your portfolio. | 4 | | |

3. **Possible Accidents and Safety Precautions:** Research and think about different accidents that might happen at your party. Use the Possible Accidents and Safety Precautions organizer (attached) to list at least three possible accidents that may occur. Next, create and record at least two precaution ideas for each of these accidents. Include this organizer as the next page in your portfolio. | 3 | | |

Weeks 8 and 9: Remaining Portfolio Materials and Exhibit (12 points)

1. **Table of Contents:** Create a table of contents that lists all the pages of your portfolio along with their page numbers. | 2 | | |

2. **Cover Page:** Create an eye-catching cover page for your portfolio that includes a creative title for your project as well as your name and the Classroom Presentation date. | 2 | | |

3. **Portfolio:** Organize all of your materials into a three-ring binder. The table of contents should be first, followed by your project work from each week in the order presented. Your cover page should be on the front of your portfolio. | 2 | | |

4. **Display Board:** Use a large two- or three-panel display board to showcase your project. It must include your project's title and your name. Remember to include your theme choice party hat, community map, food and drink budget poster and serving area illustration on your display board. You may then choose to add copies of any of your portfolio items or any additional materials that you wish. | 3 | | |

5. **Exhibit:** Arrange your portfolio, theme banner, theme picture book choice, party craft model, computer-created invitation and any additional materials you wish to include in an appealing and informative way. | 3 | | |

TEACHER ASSESSMENT

Week 10: Classroom Presentation (8 points)

1. Your Presentation • Party Type and Theme (1 point): Share your party type and theme. • Game or Craft (2 points): Explain and show your game or craft. • Book Talk (5 points): Reread the book you chose as your favorite picture book choice. Choose a section from the book (two to three paragraphs) that would be enjoyable to share with others. Next, practice reading the paragraphs out loud until you can read them smoothly and clearly. For your presentation book talk: • Read the book's title and author. Show the cover of the book. • Read aloud the section you chose and practiced. • Share your reasons that others should read this book. Remember that you already recorded reasons on your Theme Picture Book Choices organizer.	8		
TOTAL PROJECT POINTS	**100**		

STUDENT SELF-ASSESSMENT

PARTY PLAN
100 total possible for the project.

Requirements	Possible Points	Student Points
Week 1: Party Type (9 points)		
1. Party Type Balloon Brainstorm: Think about different events in life that you might like to celebrate. Using your Balloon Brainstorm organizer (attached), write various types of parties you might like to have to celebrate these events. Record one type of party on each balloon, using at least five of the balloons.	2	
2. Party Type Balloon Color Ranking: Choose three different colors of crayons, pencils or markers. Now choose one of those colors for your best ideas, a second color for your second choice ideas and a third color for your least favorite ideas. Record them on your Balloon Brainstorm organizer. Color each balloon on your Balloon Brainstorm organizer according to your color key. Leave a small amount of white around the words in your balloons so they can be read. To help make your coloring decisions, think about why you might enjoy one party more than another.	3	
3. Party Type Balloon Choice: Read your Best Idea colored balloons and from those, choose the party idea that you think would be the most exciting to plan. On your Balloon Brainstorm organizer, outline your party choice balloon with a new color that makes it stand out. This will be the party you plan for this project. Include your finished Balloon Brainstorm organizer as the first page in your portfolio.	1	
4. Computer-Created Bullet Point Reasons: Use the computer and title a new document, "I chose this party because..." Next, use bullet points to list at least four reasons you chose the party you did. You may also include reasons for not choosing your other party ideas. Include this as the second page in your portfolio.	3	
Week 2: Party Theme (15 points)		
1. Theme Idea Labels: Using your Theme Idea Labels organizer (attached), write five or more different themes that you might choose for your party. Follow the organizer directions to rank and record your idea labels. Save these labels for the "Theme Choice Party Hat" step, below.	2	
2. Theme Choice Party Hat: Cut out each of your Theme Idea Labels. Glue the labels onto the Theme Choice Party Hat organizer (attached) in order, so your favorite theme is in the party hat pompon and your least favorite theme idea is in the bottom stripe of the hat. Color your party hat leaving the labels white. The theme idea in your party hat's pompon will be the theme for your party. Cut out your finalized party hat and save it to attach to your final display board. You may also want to make a copy of your hat to include in your portfolio.	3	

STUDENT SELF-ASSESSMENT

3. Theme Party Banner: Design a banner that celebrates your party and party theme. Be sure to include the type of party it is. Write words and draw pictures that go along with your theme. Make it festive and be creative! Save your finished banner to use as part of your final exhibit.	5	
4. Theme Picture Book Choices: Locate at least three fiction or non fiction picture books related to your theme. Using the Theme Picture Book Choices organizer, record the book titles and the name of each book's author. Read the books and choose your favorite. Record your favorite book choice and write at least three reasons why you think other people should read this book. Include this as the next page in your portfolio.	5	
Week 3: Party Details and Strategies (7 points)		
1. Party Planning Guide I: Using the Party Planning Guide I organizer (attached), think about and research different options for the sections listed. For each section, make a decision and record it. Include your finished guide as the next page in your portfolio.	3	
2. Environmental Strategies: Use the Environmental Strategies organizer (attached) to create ways of reducing, reusing and recycling at your party. Add your completed Environmental Strategies organizer as the next page in your portfolio.	4	
Week 4: Party Activities and Details (16 points)		
1. Party Game: Invent a party game that relates to your theme. Complete the Party Game organizer (attached) and include its two pages as the next pages in your portfolio.	6	
2. Craft Creation and Model: Design a craft your party guests can make and take home with them. Your craft should relate to your party theme. Save your craft model for part of your final project exhibit. Use the Craft Creation organizer (attached) to record your craft idea and directions. Include its two pages as the next pages in your portfolio.	8	
3. Party Planning Guide II: Use the Party Planning Guide II organizer (attached) to think about different options for the party planning sections listed. For each section, make a decision and record it. Add this finished organizer as the next page in your portfolio.	2	

STUDENT SELF-ASSESSMENT

Week 5: Party Mailings (9 points)

1. **Computer-Created Invitation:** Using the computer, design and write an invitation for your party. Be sure that the invitation design relates to your theme. Use both of your Party Planning Guides and make sure you include the starred information from them. Include a response date and contact information such as your phone number and email address. Don't use your real contact information! Instead, be creative and make up your contact information. Save your invitation for your final exhibit. You may also include an extra copy of it as the next page in your portfolio.	5	
2. **Community Map:** Draw a map of your party's location including its surrounding area with roads and landmarks. Include a map key and a compass rose. Save this for your final display board. You may also include an extra copy of this as the next page in your portfolio.	4	

Week 6: Party Fare (14 points)

1. **Food and Drink Budget Poster:** At the top of a poster or large sheet of paper, record the title, "Party Food and Drink Choices." Below your title, record the number of party guests you will be inviting. Next, divide your poster into two equal sections, one labeled, "Food," and one labeled, "Drinks". Look through sale ads from grocery stores and choose five or six foods that you would enjoy serving at your party. Cut each food choice from the paper with its price. Arrange the pictures so they are equally spaced on the "Food" side of your poster. Using a party food budget of $15 total, calculate the cost to buy enough of each food item. Record the total cost with each item. Circle the food you will buy for your party, making sure it is within your food budget. Repeat this process using the other side of your poster for your party drinks. Your party drink budget is $10 total. Save the poster for your final display board.	6	
2. **Serving Plan Chart:** Look over your snack and drink choices. Decide what types of serving supplies you will need. This includes items you need to serve and items your guests will need to enjoy your snacks and drinks. Create your own chart that shows the serving items needed, the number of each needed and each item's use. Include this as the next page in your portfolio.	4	
3. **Serving Area Illustration:** Decide where you will serve your party snacks and drinks. Draw a picture of your serving area. Be sure to include your snacks, drinks and serving pieces. Label the items in your illustration. Be creative with color, photos, stickers, magazine clippings or other ideas. Save this for your final display board. You may also want to make a copy of your illustration to include in your portfolio.	4	

STUDENT SELF-ASSESSMENT

Week 7: Finishing Touches (10 points)

1. **Sequence of Preparations and Events:** Use the two Sequence of Preparations and Events organizers (attached) to plan the order in which you will do things for and at your party. Include the completed Sequence of Preparations and Events II organizer as the next page in your portfolio.	3	
2. **Weather Adjustments:** Research the average weather patterns for your party location at the time of year you will have your party. Using the Weather Adjustments organizer, record this information with the heading, "Weather Patterns." Be sure to write the source for where you found your information. Next, explain how you think these weather patterns might affect your party. Last, describe at least two party adjustments you may need to make due to weather that may occur. Include this organizer as the next page in your portfolio.	4	
3. **Possible Accidents and Safety Precautions:** Research and think about different accidents that might happen at your party. Use the Possible Accidents and Safety Precautions organizer (attached) to list at least three possible accidents that may occur. Next, create and record at least two precaution ideas for each of these accidents. Include this organizer as the next page in your portfolio.	3	

Weeks 8 and 9: Remaining Portfolio Materials and Exhibit (12 points)

1. **Table of Contents:** Create a table of contents that lists all the pages of your portfolio along with their page numbers.	2	
2. **Cover Page:** Create an eye-catching cover page for your portfolio that includes a creative title for your project as well as your name and the Classroom Presentation date.	2	
3. **Portfolio:** Organize all of your materials into a three-ring binder. The table of contents should be first, followed by your project work from each week in the order presented. Your cover page should be on the front of your portfolio.	2	
4. **Display Board:** Use a large two- or three-panel display board to showcase your project. It must include your project's title and your name. Remember to include your theme choice party hat, community map, food and drink budget poster and serving area illustration on your display board. You may then choose to add copies of any of your portfolio items or any additional materials that you wish.	3	
5. **Exhibit:** Arrange your portfolio, theme banner, theme picture book choice, party craft model, computer-created invitation and any additional materials you wish to include in an appealing and informative way.	3	

STUDENT SELF-ASSESSMENT

Week 10: Classroom Presentation (8 points)

1. Your Presentation • Party Type and Theme (1 point): Share your party type and theme. • Game or Craft (2 points): Explain and show your game or craft. • Book Talk (5 points): Reread the book you chose as your favorite picture book choice. Choose a section from the book (two to three paragraphs) that would be enjoyable to share with others. Next, practice reading the paragraphs out loud until you can read them smoothly and clearly. For your presentation book talk: • Read the book's title and author. Show the cover of the book. • Read aloud the section you chose and practiced. • Share your reasons that others should read this book. Remember that you already recorded reasons on your Theme Picture Book Choices organizer.	8	
TOTAL PROJECT POINTS	**100**	

STUDENT POST PROJECT REFLECTION

Student Name: _____ Reflection Date: _____

Party Type: _____ Party Theme: _____

directions

Think about your project and answer the questions below.

questions

1. Did you try your best on all parts of your project? Please explain.

   _____

   _____

2. What would you change about your project if you could? Please explain.

   _____

   _____

3. How can you work better for your next Envision project? Please explain.

   _____

   _____

4. What did you learn about yourself by working on this project? Please explain.

   _____

   _____

5. Did you enjoy creating this project? Why or why not?

   _____

   _____

APPENDIX 2: PARTY PLAN RESOURCE CARDS FOR STUDENTS

RESOURCE CARDS WEEK 1

PARTY TYPE BALLOON BRAINSTORM

People have parties for many reasons. Common types of parties are for holidays or celebrations such as birthday parties. Some people like to have creative types of parties such as a party to raise money for a cause or a party to celebrate an event like losing a first tooth.

Your party can be a common type of party or a creative type of party. Brainstorm party ideas that are meaningful to you and that you might have fun planning. Try to come up with many ideas so that your brain has a chance to be creative, and you will have a great experience planning your party.

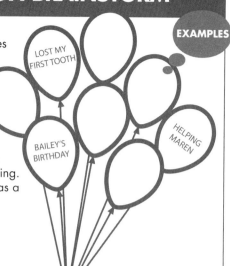

EXAMPLES: LOST MY FIRST TOOTH, BAILEY'S BIRTHDAY, HELPING MAREN

COMPUTER-CREATED BULLET POINT REASONS

Bullet points are small dots used to show listed items. Bullet points make lists easier for people to read and understand quickly. Your typing program may have a little picture showing bullet points that you can click on or it may have a word at the top such as, "Insert" or, "Edit." Look for something that says *bullets* or *special characters* to format your bullets. You can also try typing the word, "bullets" into your "Help" tool, which is usually written at the top of your typing program's screen. There may be different ways to create bullets in one typing program. Try to figure out how to do this on your own before asking for help.

EXAMPLE

I chose this party because...
- I love to _____.
- I think that my friends will _____.
- I have always wanted to _____.
- I didn't think that _____.

RESOURCE CARDS WEEK 2

THEME IDEA LABELS

A theme is a simple topic that adds excitement and unity to an event. It is usually something you like or is related to the type of party you are having. For example, if you are having a Celebration of Learning party, you might choose books for your theme. If you are having a First Day of Spring party, you might choose baby animals as your theme. Some theme examples are: pirates, puppies, baseball, western, the color green, a character, a specific movie or a specific book. Be creative with your theme, and choose one that you and your party guests will enjoy.

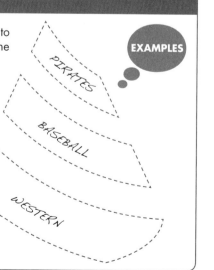

EXAMPLES: PIRATES, BASEBALL, WESTERN

Copyright © 2012 by Melanie L. Bondy, ENVISION: PARTY PLAN, Mind Vine Press, LLC. This page may be photocopied according to the official copyright guidelines at the front of this book.

THEME PARTY BANNER

A party banner is a large, usually long piece of paper or material. Party banners typically have a welcoming title that celebrates the party and its theme. Banners are not always at a party, but they add excitement to it. Your party banner must have words and pictures that go along with your party and theme. Be creative and have fun with it!

EXAMPLE

RESOURCE CARD WEEK 3

ENVIRONMENTAL STRATEGIES

EXAMPLES

Reduce: To use less.
I reduce by using less toothpaste.

Reuse: To use again.
I reuse by turning my cup into a vase.

Recycle: To use machines and change one thing into another.
I recycle by taking my empty cans back to the store.

Your environment includes everything around you! Trees, animals, air, land, water – even houses are all part of your environment. Environmental strategies can help your community be friendlier to the environment and make our world a better place to live. On the left is a chart of three environmentally friendly practices.

RESOURCE CARDS WEEK 4

PARTY GAME

Most people love to play games, and what better occasion than at a party? When creating your party game, think about the age and abilities of your guests, the amount of time you'll have to play and the materials you'll need. Keep the rules and materials simple so that it's easy to manage.

Your game can be a hunt, a sitting game, an active game or even a game with just words. When you come up with an idea, try playing the game in your mind and imagine whether or not it will be fun. You'll also need to decide on the object of the game. The **object** of the game is the goal that the players need to accomplish to win the game.

Once you've come up with your game's object, try playing it with your family or some friends. This will help you figure out how to set-up, how to play, the rules and the supplies needed. Have fun playing!

CRAFT CREATION AND MODEL

Crafts are handmade projects created with everyday materials. Some material ideas may be: foil, popsicle sticks, material scraps, construction paper, buttons, pipe cleaners, magazine clippings, portions of cereal boxes or cotton balls.

Your craft should be fun and simple enough for your guests to complete in about ten minutes. Consider their age and interests.

There are two options for deciding on a craft. One option is, with permission, gather materials you have at home or school. Next, combine the materials in a creative way to make your own original craft. A second option is to invent your craft idea first. Then, with permission, gather materials you have at home or school and create your craft.

Once you've created a craft that you are happy with, complete the Craft Creation organizer.

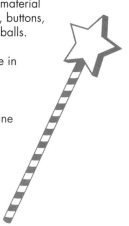

RESOURCE CARDS
WEEK 5

COMPUTER-CREATED INVITATION

A party invitation is usually given to each guest invited to a party. A party invitation will create excitement about your party and provide your guests with important details about your party.

Your invitation should be appealing, neat and creative. Be sure to illustrate it to represent your theme. It should include the reason for your party. It should also list the date, time and location of your party. If your guests need to bring, wear or know anything special for your party, be sure to write that information as well.

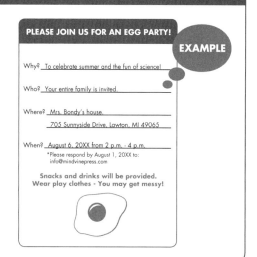

EXAMPLE

PLEASE JOIN US FOR AN EGG PARTY!

Why? To celebrate summer and the fun of science!
Who? Your entire family is invited.
Where? Mrs. Bondy's house.
705 Sunnyside Drive, Lawton, MI 49065
When? August 6, 20XX from 2 p.m. - 4 p.m.
*Please respond by August 1, 20XX to: info@mindvinepress.com

Snacks and drinks will be provided.
Wear play clothes - You may get messy!

COMMUNITY MAP

A map is a visual likeness of a place or area. It is a good idea to include a map to your party location with each invitation so that your guests can find your party easily. Maps need to be neat, easy to read and contain enough information for readers to understand them. Be sure to include a map key, a compass rose and important community features that your guests will recognize.

A **map key** explains symbols used on a map. It is usually placed at the side or bottom of the map in a small box. A basic **compass rose** has arrows showing where the directions north, south, east and west are on the map.

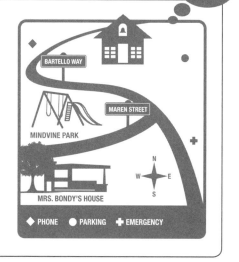

EXAMPLE

Resource Cards
WEEK 6

FOOD AND DRINK BUDGET POSTER

Most parties include some type of food and drink. Some include a full meal while others offer snacks. Be creative as you research food ideas for your party. You might find foods related to your theme.

To calculate the cost for party food and drinks, you will need to follow a few steps:

1. Read the number of servings the item's package contains.
2. Divide your number of guests by the number of servings in the package. If your answer is a decimal, round up to the next whole number. This is the number of packages you would need to buy.
3. Next, multiply the number of packages needed to buy by the price of each package. This is the total cost to buy that item for your party.

PARTIAL EXAMPLE

Party Food and Drink Choices
Number of party guests: 12

Food
- 8 Servings $6.00
- 2 Packages Needed
- Total Cost $12.00

Drinks
- 10 Servings $4.00
- 2 Packages Needed
- Total Cost $8.00

SERVING PLAN CHART

A chart is a visual way to organize information. Creating a serving plan chart will help make sure you have all the supplies needed to serve your food and drinks. As you make your chart, think about each item you will serve. Picture yourself serving the item. What will you serve it with? What will you serve it on? What will your guests use to eat or drink the item? Imagining will help make sure you have listed all the items you will need.

PARTY SERVING PLAN

PARTIAL EXAMPLE

SERVING ITEM	#	Usage
LARGE KNIFE	1	To cut cake
SPATULA	1	To serve cake
PAPER PLATES	15	To eat cake
NAPKINS	15	To use with cake
FORKS	15	To eat cake
CUPS	15	To drink lemonade

SERVING AREA ILLUSTRATION

An illustration is a colored drawing. Creating an illustration of your serving area will help you plan enough room for your snacks, drinks and serving pieces. It will also save time on the day of your event when you are setting up. In addition, your illustration will show others how you visualize this aspect of your party.

You may want to illustrate your platform (a table, for example) first. Next, illustrate and label your food, drinks and serving items on a separate sheet of paper. You can then cut them out and arrange them before gluing them onto your serving area.

PARTIAL EXAMPLE

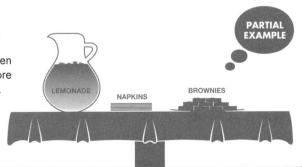

RESOURCE CARDS
WEEKS 8-9

TABLE OF CONTENTS

A table of contents is a list of sections and page numbers at the beginning of a book. Its purpose is to show the book's main topics and where to find them. Your table of contents should be the first page in your portfolio. List the title of each section in your portfolio and the page number on which each section begins. It should be neat and well organized, but feel free to be creative with your own layout.

PARTIAL EXAMPLE

TABLE OF CONTENTS

Page Number	Section Title
1	Balloon Brainstorm Organizer
2	Computer-Created Bullet Point Reasons
3	Theme Choice Party Hat
4	Theme Picture Book Choices Organizer

COVER PAGE AND PORTFOLIO

The cover page of your portfolio should entice people to read about your project. It should include an original title, your name and the Classroom Presentation date. Your portfolio is used to organize most of your paper items. A one- to two-inch binder with a clear cover works well. Arrange your papers in the order listed in your Student Instruction Guide. You may choose to add tab dividers, page protectors and creative touches.

FRONT COVER    SPINE    BACK COVER

EXAMPLE

DISPLAY BOARD AND EXHIBIT

The purpose of your display board and exhibit is to draw people's attention to your project. It should be neat, colorful and creative. You should include the items listed in your Student Instruction Guide and any additional materials you wish to bring. The example below is to be used only as a guide; feel free to rearrange. Tip: two- or three-panel display boards can be purchased at most craft stores. If you would prefer to make one, you can ask an adult to help construct one from a large cardboard box.

EXAMPLE

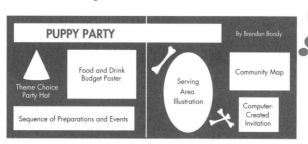

**RESOURCE CARD
WEEK 10**

YOUR PRESENTATION

Your presentation will be about what you learned, collected and made for your project. It will also include your book talk. You should practice until you are comfortable with what you will say, but do not memorize a speech. Your presentation should be three to four minutes long. Be sure to include the bulleted information listed in Week 10 of your Student Instruction Guide.

REMEMBER TO:
- Take a deep breath, relax and enjoy sharing.
- Greet your audience and introduce yourself.
- Speak clearly, loudly enough so everyone can hear you, and at a natural pace.
- Stand still and calm; don't fidget.
- Point to and show various items as you speak about them.
- Make eye contact with your audience, looking around the room naturally.
- Thank your audience when you are finished.

APPENDIX 3: SPANISH TRANSLATIONS OF PARENT FORMS

envision® carta de introduccción

Estimados Padres,

Tengo el placer de informarles que su hijo/a ha sido seleccionado/a para participar en el Programa Académico de Educación Avanzada llamado Envision. El motivo de la presente es para explicarle el programa y para solicitar su permiso para que su hijo/a pueda participar en esta oportunidad muy especial.

Envision es un programa extraordinario diseñado para aquellos estudiantes cuyas habilidades no están siendo satisfechas con el currículo usual de su nivel académico. Este programa se enfoca en el desarrollo del pensamiento crítico y la creatividad. El programa guía a los estudiantes a utilizar proyectos basados en la vida real que los motivara a descubrir como pueden alzcanzar sus metas personales en el futuro.

Su hijo/a ha sido invitado a participar en el Proyecto Fiesta, el cual permite a los estudiantes planificar una fiesta con un tema para celebrar un evento especial.

Los estudiantes trabajarán con Envision durante el tiempo de clase, su tiempo libre y en la casa.

Para que su hijo/a participe en Envision por favor llene la porción al final de esta carta titulada "Formulario de Participación" y regrésela tan pronto sea posible. Si a usted le gustaría que su hijo/a participe en Envision, por favor lea la carta adjunta titulada Carta de Introducción para Padres del Projecto Fiesta. Esta carta le informará sobre el proyecto, fechas importantes, y le pedirá su autorización de participación.

Envision será una oportunidad de aprendizaje estupenda para su hijo/a. Espero que su hijo/a participe en este programa,y si tiene preguntas por favor no dude de ponerse en contacto conmigo.

Sinceramente,

_____

_____

---

envision® formulario de participación

Por favor complete esta forma y envíela lo más pronto posible. Fecha: _____

☐ He leído la carta de Introducción para Padres de Envision y le doy permiso a mi hijo/a para participar en el programa Envision.

☐ He leído la carta de Introducción para Padres de Envision y no le doy permiso a mi hijo/a para participar en el programa Envision.

Nombre del Estudiante: _____ Firma de Padre: _____

carta de padres para el proyecto fiesta

Estimados Padres,

Bienvenidos a "Fiesta", un proyecto del programa de Envision. Esperamos que este proyecto sea un reto y una inspiración para su hijo/a. El proyecto "Fiesta" inmediatamente sumergirá al estudiante en el reto de planificar una fiesta temática para celebrar un evento especial.

Para este proyecto, su hijo/a escogerá un evento para celebrar y para incorporar un tema en su fiesta. Después, su hijo creará un rótulo estilo "banner" para la fiesta y leerá libros relacionados con el tema de la fiesta. Su hijo también creará un juego para la fiesta, una manualidad, una invitación, un mapa, un cartel de comida y bebida, una ilustración indicando donde será la comida servida y mucho más. Todos estos materiales serán coleccionados en un portafolio. Continuando, el estudiante creará y diseñará una exhibición cual capturará los puntos claves de su proyecto Fiesta. Por último, su hijo/a presentará su proyecto a la clase y participará en un "expo" de proyectos.

Una Guía Estudiantil será proveída semanalmente para orientar al estudiante paso por paso y guiarlo por este proceso. La Guía Estudiantil es una lista completa que indica los requisitos de este proyecto y está diseñada a guiar al alumno a que comience a pensar usando un nivel superior. Junto con esta guía, su hijo recibirá organizadores del proyecto que corresponden con ciertos rectos requeridos. La guía también menciona las Tarjetas de Recursos que proveen explicaciones adicionales, ideas, consejos, y otros informes. Estas tarjetas también estarán disponibles en el salón de su hijo/a para el uso de él/ella.

El proyecto Fiesta está diseñado para que el alumno pueda trabajar independientemente en su salón, durante su tiempo libre y en casa. Varias "Juntas de Reviso" están programadas durante el proyecto para que yo esté al pendiente del progreso del estudiante. En las fechas indicadas, el estudiante y yo nos reuniremos para discutir sus logros y para planear nuevas metas para la siguiente junta. También, veremos si el estudiante ha tenido dificultades o si tiene algunas preguntas.

El proyecto Fiesta se terminará en un "Expo de Proyectos". Este expo dará una oportunidad al estudiante a que comparta su trabajo y sus experiencias con su familia, amigos, e invitados. Usted recibirá una invitación para el "Expo de Proyectos" en una fecha futura.

Fechas para Recordar:

Reviso 1: _____ **Reviso 2:** _____

Reviso 3: _____ **Presentación:** _____

Expo del Proyecto "Fiesta": _____, _____

Sinceramente,

_____

_____

CONTRATO DE COMPROMISO ESTUDIANTIL

expectativas

tiempo de proyecto

Acepto:
- seguir los pasos indicados en mi guía estudiantil mientras que hago mi trabajo.
- mantener en orden mis materiales de proyecto.
- trabajar duro en Envision sin molestar a otros.
- mantener mis preguntas para mi mismo, hasta que mi maestro/a esté libre para hablar.

juntas de reviso

Estaré preparado con:
- mi Guía Estudiantil.
- mi Organizador Estudiantil.
- todos los materiales necesitados para el proyecto.

fechas importantes

Reviso 1: _____   Presentación a la Clase: _____

Reviso 2: _____   Expo Proyecto Fiesta: _____

Reviso 3: _____   _____

firmas

Acepto:
- cumplir con las expectativas en las fechas citadas anteriormente.
- completar todos los requisitos del proyecto lo mejor que yo pueda.
- traer mi proyecto a la escuela todos los días, así podré trabajar en él durante mi tiempo libre.
- llevar mi proyecto a la casa todos los días, así podré trabajar en casa.

Comprendo que este proyecto de Envision es una oportunidad muy especial, y si no lleno los requisitos explicados anteriormente, existe la posibilidad de que no pueda proseguir y tenga que retornar a las actividades normales del salón.

Firma Estudiantil: _____   Fecha: _____

Firma de Padre: _____   Fecha: _____

Por favor devuelva este contrato antes de: _____

¡ESTÁ INVITADO!

¡POR FAVOR, ACOMPÁÑENOS EN EL "EXPO" PROJECTO FIESTA DE ENVISION!

¿Por qué? _____

¿Quién? _____

¿Adónde? _____

¿Cuándo? _____

¡Recuerde de traer su cámara!

RESPUESTA AL "EXPO"

Por favor complete y regrese antes de: _____

Nombre del estudiante: _____

¿El estudiante estará presente? ☐ Sí ☐ No

¿Número de invitados? _____

¿El estudiante necesitará equipo especial para su "expo" (p. ej. una Tele)? Por favor escriba lo necesario: _____

Gracias.

Esperamos contar con su presencia durante este evento especial.

APPENDIX 4: ADDITIONAL INFORMATION

ABOUT THE AUTHOR

Melanie Bondy taught elementary students for seven years before authoring the Envision program. She has always had a special interest in challenging students to reach their highest potential while making learning relevant and fun. When she saw a widespread need for higher quality materials for gifted students, she utilized her talents to create this unique educational program.

After publishing Envision programs for grades three, four and five, Melanie is thrilled to introduce Envision Singles to educators everywhere. The success of Envision has been overwhelming and its reviews have been purely positive. Melanie is planning to produce numerous Envision Singles appropriate for students in grades one through eight.

Melanie is a popular speaker in several states and has spoken at numerous educational conferences nationwide. She has also consulted with many school districts across the nation. Melanie is happy to discuss the presentation of the Envision program to teachers in your district.

Feel free to contact Melanie Bondy c/o:
Mind Vine Press
6818 Calm Meadow Drive
Frisco, TX 75035
Phone: 269.978.7227
Fax: 269.978.6871
Email: melanie@mindvinepress.com
www.mindvinepress.com

APPENDIX 5: PARTY PLAN RESOURCE CARDS FOR THE CLASSROOM

PARTY TYPE BALLOON BRAINSTORM

People have parties for many reasons. Common types of parties are for holidays or celebrations such as birthday parties. Some people like to have creative types of parties such as a party to raise money for a cause or a party to celebrate an event like losing a first tooth.

Your party can be a common type of party or a creative type of party. Brainstorm party ideas that are meaningful to you and that you might have fun planning. Try to come up with many ideas so that your brain has a chance to be creative, and you will have a great experience planning your party.

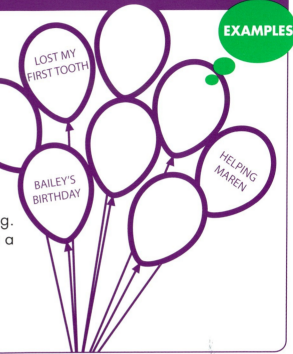

EXAMPLES: LOST MY FIRST TOOTH, BAILEY'S BIRTHDAY, HELPING MAREN

Copyright © 2012 by Melanie L. Bondy, ENVISION: PARTY PLAN, Mind Vine Press, LLC. This card may not be photocopied.

COMPUTER-CREATED BULLET POINT REASONS

Bullet points are small dots used to show listed items. Bullet points make lists easier for people to read and understand quickly. Your typing program may have a little picture showing bullet points that you can click on or it may have a word at the top such as, "Insert" or, "Edit." Look for something that says *bullets* or *special characters* to format your bullets. You can also try typing the word, "bullets" into your "Help" tool, which is usually written at the top of your typing program's screen. There may be different ways to create bullets in one typing program. Try to figure out how to do this on your own before asking for help.

I chose this party because... (EXAMPLE)

- I love to _____.
- I think that my friends will _____.
- I have always wanted to _____.
- I didn't think that _____.

Copyright © 2012 by Melanie L. Bondy, ENVISION: PARTY PLAN, Mind Vine Press, LLC. This card may not be photocopied.

THEME IDEA LABELS

A theme is a simple topic that adds excitement and unity to an event. It is usually something you like or is related to the type of party you are having. For example, if you are having a Celebration of Learning party, you might choose books for your theme. If you are having a First Day of Spring party, you might choose baby animals as your theme. Some theme examples are: pirates, puppies, baseball, western, the color green, a character, a specific movie or a specific book. Be creative with your theme, and choose one that you and your party guests will enjoy.

EXAMPLES

- PIRATES
- BASEBALL
- WESTERN

Copyright © 2012 by Melanie L. Bondy, ENVISION: PARTY PLAN, Mind Vine Press, LLC. This card may not be photocopied.

THEME PARTY BANNER

A party banner is a large, usually long piece of paper or material. Party banners typically have a welcoming title that celebrates the party and its theme. Banners are not always at a party, but they add excitement to it. Your party banner must have words and pictures that go along with your party and theme. Be creative and have fun with it!

EXAMPLE

WELCOME TO BAILEY'S BACKYARD BARBECUE!

Copyright © 2012 by Melanie L. Bondy, ENVISION: PARTY PLAN, Mind Vine Press, LLC. This card may not be photocopied.

ENVIRONMENTAL STRATEGIES

EXAMPLES

Reduce: To use less.
I reduce by using less toothpaste.

Reuse: To use again.
I reuse by turning my cup into a vase.

Recycle: To use machines and change one thing into another.
I recycle by taking my empty cans back to the store.

Your environment includes everything around you! Trees, animals, air, land, water – even houses are all part of your environment. Environmental strategies can help your community be friendlier to the environment and make our world a better place to live. On the left is a chart of three environmentally friendly practices.

Copyright © 2012 by Melanie L. Bondy, ENVISION: PARTY PLAN, Mind Vine Press, LLC. This card may not be photocopied.

PARTY GAME

Most people love to play games, and what better occasion than at a party? When creating your party game, think about the age and abilities of your guests, the amount of time you'll have to play and the materials you'll need. Keep the rules and materials simple so that it's easy to manage.

Your game can be a hunt, a sitting game, an active game or even a game with just words. When you come up with an idea, try playing the game in your mind and imagine whether or not it will be fun. You'll also need to decide on the object of the game. The **object** of the game is the goal that the players need to accomplish to win the game.

Once you've come up with your game's object, try playing it with your family or some friends. This will help you figure out how to set-up, how to play, the rules and the supplies needed. Have fun playing!

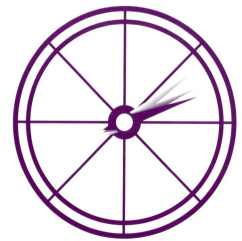

Copyright © 2012 by Melanie L. Bondy, ENVISION: PARTY PLAN, Mind Vine Press, LLC. This card may not be photocopied.

CRAFT CREATION AND MODEL

Crafts are handmade projects created with everyday materials. Some material ideas may be: foil, popsicle sticks, material scraps, construction paper, buttons, pipe cleaners, magazine clippings, portions of cereal boxes or cotton balls.

Your craft should be fun and simple enough for your guests to complete in about ten minutes. Consider their age and interests.

There are two options for deciding on a craft. One option is, with permission, gather materials you have at home or school. Next, combine the materials in a creative way to make your own original craft. A second option is to invent your craft idea first. Then, with permission, gather materials you have at home or school and create your craft.

Once you've created a craft that you are happy with, complete the Craft Creation organizer.

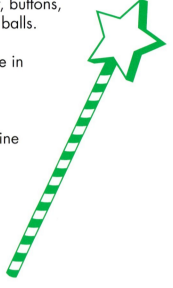

Copyright © 2012 by Melanie L. Bondy, ENVISION: PARTY PLAN, Mind Vine Press, LLC. This card may not be photocopied.

COMPUTER-CREATED INVITATION

A party invitation is usually given to each guest invited to a party. A party invitation will create excitement about your party and provide your guests with important details about your party.

Your invitation should be appealing, neat and creative. Be sure to illustrate it to represent your theme. It should include the reason for your party. It should also list the date, time and location of your party. If your guests need to bring, wear or know anything special for your party, be sure to write that information as well.

Copyright © 2012 by Melanie L. Bondy, ENVISION: PARTY PLAN, Mind Vine Press, LLC. This card may not be photocopied.

COMMUNITY MAP

EXAMPLE

A map is a visual likeness of a place or area. It is a good idea to include a map to your party location with each invitation so that your guests can find your party easily. Maps need to be neat, easy to read and contain enough information for readers to understand them. Be sure to include a map key, a compass rose and important community features that your guests will recognize.

A **map key** explains symbols used on a map. It is usually placed at the side or bottom of the map in a small box. A basic **compass rose** has arrows showing where the directions north, south, east and west are on the map.

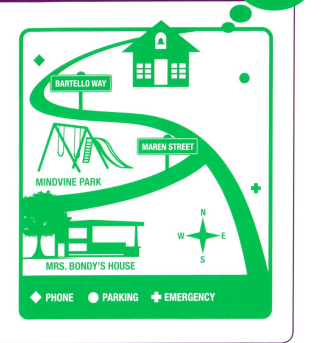

Copyright © 2012 by Melanie L. Bondy, ENVISION: PARTY PLAN, Mind Vine Press, LLC. This card may not be photocopied.

FOOD AND DRINK BUDGET POSTER

Most parties include some type of food and drink. Some include a full meal while others offer snacks. Be creative as you research food ideas for your party. You might find foods related to your theme.

To calculate the cost for party food and drinks, you will need to follow a few steps:

1. Read the number of servings the item's package contains.
2. Divide your number of guests by the number of servings in the package. If your answer is a decimal, round up to the next whole number. This is the number of packages you would need to buy.
3. Next, multiply the number of packages needed to buy by the price of each package. This is the total cost to buy that item for your party.

PARTIAL EXAMPLE

Copyright © 2012 by Melanie L. Bondy, ENVISION: PARTY PLAN, Mind Vine Press, LLC. This card may not be photocopied.

SERVING PLAN CHART

A chart is a visual way to organize information. Creating a serving plan chart will help make sure you have all the supplies needed to serve your food and drinks. As you make your chart, think about each item you will serve. Picture yourself serving the item. What will you serve it with? What will you serve it on? What will your guests use to eat or drink the item? Imagining will help make sure you have listed all the items you will need.

PARTIAL EXAMPLE

PARTY SERVING PLAN

SERVING ITEM	#	Usage
LARGE KNIFE	1	To cut cake
SPATULA	1	To serve cake
PAPER PLATES	15	To eat cake
NAPKINS	15	To use with cake
FORKS	15	To eat cake
CUPS	15	To drink lemonade

Copyright © 2012 by Melanie L. Bondy, ENVISION: PARTY PLAN, Mind Vine Press, LLC. This card may not be photocopied.

SERVING AREA ILLUSTRATION

An illustration is a colored drawing. Creating an illustration of your serving area will help you plan enough room for your snacks, drinks and serving pieces. It will also save time on the day of your event when you are setting up. In addition, your illustration will show others how you visualize this aspect of your party.

You may want to illustrate your platform (a table, for example) first. Next, illustrate and label your food, drinks and serving items on a separate sheet of paper. You can then cut them out and arrange them before gluing them onto your serving area.

PARTIAL EXAMPLE

Copyright © 2012 by Melanie L. Bondy, ENVISION: PARTY PLAN, Mind Vine Press, LLC. This card may not be photocopied.

TABLE OF CONTENTS

A table of contents is a list of sections and page numbers at the beginning of a book. Its purpose is to show the book's main topics and where to find them. Your table of contents should be the first page in your portfolio. List the title of each section in your portfolio and the page number on which each section begins. It should be neat and well organized, but feel free to be creative with your own layout.

PARTIAL EXAMPLE

TABLE OF CONTENTS

Page Number	Section Title
1	Balloon Brainstorm Organizer
2	Computer-Created Bullet Point Reasons
3	Theme Choice Party Hat
4	Theme Picture Book Choices Organizer

Copyright © 2012 by Melanie L. Bondy, ENVISION: PARTY PLAN, Mind Vine Press, LLC. This card may not be photocopied.

COVER PAGE AND PORTFOLIO

The cover page of your portfolio should entice people to read about your project. It should include an original title, your name and the Classroom Presentation date. Your portfolio is used to organize most of your paper items. A one- to two-inch binder with a clear cover works well. Arrange your papers in the order listed in your Student Instruction Guide. You may choose to add tab dividers, page protectors and creative touches.

EXAMPLE

Copyright © 2012 by Melanie L. Bondy, ENVISION: PARTY PLAN, Mind Vine Press, LLC. This card may not be photocopied.

DISPLAY BOARD AND EXHIBIT

The purpose of your display board and exhibit is to draw people's attention to your project. It should be neat, colorful and creative. You should include the items listed in your Student Instruction Guide and any additional materials you wish to bring. The example below is to be used only as a guide; feel free to rearrange. Tip: two- or three-panel display boards can be purchased at most craft stores. If you would prefer to make one, you can ask an adult to help construct one from a large cardboard box.

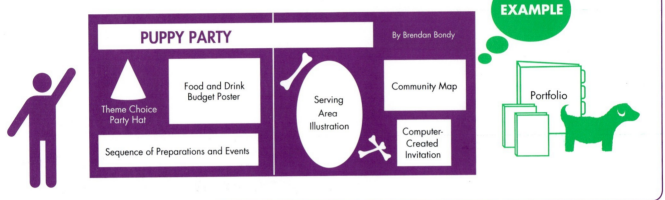

Copyright © 2012 by Melanie L. Bondy, ENVISION: PARTY PLAN, Mind Vine Press, LLC. This card may not be photocopied.

YOUR PRESENTATION

Your presentation will be about what you learned, collected and made for your project. It will also include your book talk. You should practice until you are comfortable with what you will say, but do not memorize a speech. Your presentation should be three to four minutes long. Be sure to include the bulleted information listed in Week 10 of your Student Instruction Guide.

REMEMBER TO:
- Take a deep breath, relax and enjoy sharing.
- Greet your audience and introduce yourself.
- Speak clearly, loudly enough so everyone can hear you, and at a natural pace.
- Stand still and calm; don't fidget.
- Point to and show various items as you speak about them.
- Make eye contact with your audience, looking around the room naturally.
- Thank your audience when you are finished.

Copyright © 2012 by Melanie L. Bondy, ENVISION: PARTY PLAN, Mind Vine Press, LLC. This card may not be photocopied.